BUILDING BLOCKS *for* BIBLE STUDY

About the Author

Peter Allan Verkruyse was born on December 7, 1959 in Kewanee, Illinois. He received the Bachelor of Arts degree summa cum laude from Lincoln Christian College in 1982, graduating first in his class and being elected to the Delta Epsilon Chi and Gamma Alpha Chi honor societies.

He received the Master of Arts degree in homiletics from Lincoln Christian Seminary in 1987. His thesis, "Preaching the Word: The Life, Message and Method of G. Campbell Morgan," was accepted with distinction. In 1988, he received the Master of Divinity degree in New Testament from Lincoln Christian Seminary.

He received the Master of Arts (1990) and Doctor of Philosophy (1995) degrees in Rhetorical Theory and Criticism from the Department of Speech Communication at the University of Illinois at Urbana-Champaign where he received the Marie Hochmuth Nichols Award (1992) and the Stafford Thomas Award (1993), was named to the Incomplete List of Outstanding Teachers, and studied on a research fellowship during the summer of 1993. The title of his dissertation was "The Rhetoric of Restorationism: Alexander Campbell and the Rhetoric of Affect."

Over the past fourteen years Dr. Verkruyse has served in local church staff ministries and has taught at Lincoln Christian College (Lincoln, Illinois), Danville Area Community College (Danville, Illinois), Millikin University (Decatur, Illinois), and the University of Illinois at Urbana-Champaign. He is presently the Assistant Professor of Preaching at Kentucky Christian College (Grayson, Kentucky). He has published articles in The Christian Standard and *The Christian Chronicle and presented papers at the annual convention of the Speech Communication Association. He is a member of the Speech Communication Association, the Religious Speech Communication Association, the International Society for the History of Rhetoric, and the Academy of Homiletics.*

BUILDING BLOCKS for BIBLE STUDY

LAYING A FOUNDATION FOR LIFE

PETER VERKRUYSE

COLLEGE PRESS PUBLISHING COMPANY • JOPLIN, MISSOURI

Cover Design: Daryl Williams

Library of Congress Cataloging-in-Publication Data

Verkruyse, Peter, 1959–
    Building blocks for Bible study: laying a foundation for life / Peter A.
Verkruyse.
      p.   cm.
    Includes bibliographical references.
    ISBN 0-89900-795-3 (pbk.)
    1. Bible—Textbooks.   I. Title.
BS605.2.V47 1997
220'.071—dc21   97-37540
                                                  CIP

TABLE OF CONTENTS

INTRODUCTION 7

1. THE "A.I.M." OF BIBLE STUDY 11

2. BASIC PRINCIPLES OF EXPOSITION .19

3. CHOOSING A BIBLE AND A TEXT 27

4. SURVEYING THE BACKGROUND 37

5. EXAMINING THE CONTEXT 47

6. ANALYZING THE GRAMMAR 61

7. DEFINING THE WORDS 77

8. CONSULTING THE COMMENTARIES 97

APPENDIX ONE: BIBLE STUDY SOFTWARE 109

APPENDIX TWO: NOTES TO THE EXERCISES 115

APPENDIX THREE: TEACHER HELPS AND MATERIALS 137

GLOSSARY OF TERMS 155

REFERENCE TOOLS 159

S by S . 52

95113

To Debby —

a wife of noble character

and her husband's crown

(Proverbs 31:29)

INTRODUCTION

Several people in your church probably know 2 Timothy 3:16-17 by heart. Most learned it as a "proof-text" to support their belief in the divine inspiration of the Bible. "All Scripture is God-breathed and is useful for teaching, rebuking, correcting and training in righteousness, so that the man of God may be thoroughly equipped for every good work" (NIV). When Paul wrote "All Scripture is God-breathed" he clearly affirmed his belief in the divine authorship of Scripture. Paul could hardly have chosen such a rare term as *theopneustos* by accident. It occurs only here in Scripture and seldom in all of Greek literature,[1] yet its unique combination of component parts[2] — the term for "God" (*theos*) and a form of the term for "Spirit" or "Breath" (*pneuma*) — clearly indicates that Paul had in mind not mere poetic inspiration but a creative act of God through the operation of His Spirit.

Satisfied that we have settled this issue nicely, then, we pay less attention to what follows. Yet Paul actually devotes most of his attention to what we tend to gloss over — the fact that Scripture is "useful." What is it useful for? For "teaching, rebuking, correcting and training in righteousness." And with this goal in view — "so that the man of God may be thoroughly equipped for every good work." Nowhere will we find a stronger mandate for the study of Scripture! Many church leaders operate with an "equipping" philosophy of ministry grounded in Paul's statement in Ephesians 4:11-12: "It was he who gave some to be apostles, some to be prophets, some to be evangelists, and some to be pastors and teachers, to prepare God's people for works of service" (NIV). The word here translated "prepare" (*katartismon*) is actually a cognate form of the word translated "equipped" in 2 Timothy 3:17 (*artios*). The usefulness of Scripture and the equipping of the Christian are thus intimately bound together. Those who would "prepare" or "equip" others must devote themselves to a ministry of the Word. Those who would become "equipped for every good work" must devote themselves to the study of the Word.

Peter was probably addressing new Christians when he compared their need for "the living and enduring word of God" (1 Peter 1:23, NIV) to the need for physical nourishment: "Like newborn babies, crave pure spiritual milk, so that by it you may grow up in your salvation, now that you have tasted that the Lord is good" (1 Peter 2:2-3, NIV). This manual is designed primarily for the new Christian who is ready to take the first step in learning how to "feed" himself. Since God in His wisdom has seen fit to provide some members of Christ's body with the gift of teaching (Romans 12:6-7), it is highly unlikely that any of us will ever "outgrow" the need to be taught by someone else in the church. Yet just as physical growth enables us to feed ourselves, so our spiritual growth should enable us to provide our own nourishment from Scripture.

Because this manual is designed primarily for the new Christian or beginning student, it purposely avoids technical or specialized spheres of inquiry. A working knowledge of the languages in which the Scriptures were first written has tremendous value for adding depth and precision to our understanding of God's Word. But since few new Christians or beginning students possess such skills, the lessons in this study will focus on tools and methods within reach of the student of the English Bible. An effort will be made to introduce students to those tools which permit even the beginner to explore the use of Greek and Hebrew terms. Nevertheless, the basic conviction which undergirds these lessons is that current English translations, used comparatively, serve as adequate and reliable guides for understanding the Word of God.

Also, the methods of study described in this manual assume that we study the Bible in much the same manner that we would investigate the meaning of any written text. God chose to "breathe out" his revelation in the form of "scripture," that is in the form of *graphe* or "writing." God made His Word accessible to anyone able to read texts apart from any need for special illumination, spiritual or otherwise. It is a Word commonly available to common people with common abilities.

Nevertheless, we must recognize that the Bible was written in languages different than ours, in places different than ours, in cultures different than ours and in times different than ours. Thus there is an historical and cultural distance between the original writing of Scripture and the contemporary reader. It is not impossible to close this distance, even for the beginner. But it does mean that some sustained attention to the principles for reading texts — particularly ancient texts — is important to our spiritual growth. The principles themselves are basic and generic, within the grasp of the non-specialist. These lessons seek to train students to apply them to the Bible. In sum, then, this manual makes no pretense of offering a scholarly or academic model of "exegesis."[3] It does, however, seek to preserve the integrity of such processes in describing methods that will enable the young Christian to become a better student of the English Bible.

The lessons will focus both on explaining a set of "skills" and introducing a set of "tools." Beginning with Lesson Three in this manual, a list of skills and tools will appear at the beginning of each lesson. Lesson Two will provide an overview of the basic principles for reading biblical texts. Lesson Three will survey the major English versions and study Bibles available to the student and suggest strategies for choosing texts to study.

Lessons Four through Eight will cover the reading principles individually. First, the methods and tools for a principle will be described. Next, an exercise will help you apply those methods and tools to the study of a passage of Scripture. Bible reference tools are becoming increasingly available in computer software form. Appendix One will describe some of the more popular packages now available. Appendix Two will include notes on the exercises. These notes are designed to help teachers lead discussions of the exercises or to enable readers to check their own work. Finally, Appendix Three will include helps for those who may wish to use these materials for group study.

ENDNOTES

1. J.N.D. Kelly, *A Commentary on the Pastoral Epistles* (1963; reprint, Grand Rapids: Baker, 1981), p. 203.

2. This is usually what is meant by the term "etymology."

3. A technical term meaning to "draw out" the meaning of a text.

1 THE A.I.M. OF BIBLE STUDY

What is the goal of Bible study? It seems natural for most of us to think of it quite simply in terms of "understanding the Bible" or "discovering what the Bible means." *In general,* this description is fair enough. Yet it is both possible and preferable to be more specific. Certainly, our endeavor to "understand the Bible" should be more than an academic exercise to satisfy our idle curiosities. We should desire to enhance our knowledge and experience of the God who speaks this word to us. We should hunger to explore His truth and in that truth find His will for our lives. We should thirst to grow more like His Son, to equip ourselves to serve His Son, and to find both in His Son and in His Word that which will speak to our personal life needs and ministries, as many and varied as these may be. This is enough to suggest that Bible study actually serves several purposes and is (or should be) directed toward multiple goals. The purpose of this first lesson is to describe and prioritize these various goals.

MEANING VS. SIGNIFICANCE

Before proceeding further, it may be helpful to respond directly to some of the problematic attitudes about Bible study that often become very prominent in the life of the church. Maybe you have heard it said — if not, you may hear it said — that "the Bible means different things to different people" or that "the Bible has as many meanings as there are people who read it." You may even have heard of people who resist being taught from the Bible with an excuse like, "people can make that book say anything they want." Or else maybe you have been a part of some group "study" in which each person present was asked to describe "what this passage means to you." As innocent — or as acceptable — as such ideas may seem, it is important to understand that such attitudes represent subtle but serious threats to the importance of Bible study in the life of the church.

Herein lies the problem: *if any given passage from the Bible can legitimately "mean" anything — if there is no such thing as a "valid" or "preferred" reading of a text's "meaning" — both the authority and the relevancy of the Bible are indirectly threatened.* This may seem to be a strong statement. But it is true in at least two senses. First, if a passage does not possess a meaning (singular) but *many* meanings (plural), then the Bible cannot serve as a reliable source of stable truth. The "truth" in the text constantly changes. Therefore the Bible can no longer be considered a vehicle of truth in any absolute or unchanging sense. Second, if there are as many *meanings* in the passage as there are readers, then *meaning* is determined by the reader or receiver of the text and not by the author or sender. Since the divine authority of the Bible rests in the divine authorship or inspiration of God ("All Scripture is God-breathed"), the authority of the Bible is made null and void when *meaning* is no longer determined by the author but relocated within the receiver. Individual experience is made to sit in judgment over the Bible for the Bible no longer has the authority or the ability to transcend and judge individual experience. This is why such apparently innocent attitudes ultimately represent such serious threats to the authority and relevancy of the Bible in the life of the church.

Few of the people who would make such comments, however, intend anything so deadly. In most cases, they *intend* to communicate something not only quite different but legitimate. Usually, we simply have not learned how to clearly express a subtle but crucial distinction. We throw the word "meaning" around too loosely. We are merely doing an inadequate job of communicating the belief that *while any given passage possesses a stable "**meaning**" (in the singular sense) the "**significance**" of that meaning for the life of the reader may vary (in the plural sense).* Any passage of Scripture may have a different **significance** for my life than it does for yours but this does not mean that the **meaning** of that passage changes. For example, two different individuals may be studying Jesus' parable about the Pharisee and the Tax Collector (Luke 18:10-14). Both should be able to discern that the **meaning** of the parable is probably about our need for and dependence upon the grace of God. But the **significance** of that meaning may vary according to the reader. For one who takes undue pride in his own righteousness (like the Pharisee), the parable should be taken as a challenge to humility. But for one who is acutely aware of his own inadequacies before God (like the tax collector), the parable probably offers comfort and hope. This legitimate distinction between the **meaning** of a text and the **significance** of a text is usually what people are trying to describe when making comments like those described above.

There are several important reasons to be clear about this matter, however. First, we should avoid speaking of Bible study in ways that even indirectly or unintentionally threaten the authority and relevancy of the Bible as the Word of God. Second, this crucial distinction helps us to communicate precisely what we *do* intend to say about Bible study. And finally, for our present purposes, **it helps us to understand and appreciate the various goals of Bible study.**

PRIMARY "A.I.M."

How is this the case? Earlier we affirmed that Bible study serves several purposes and is directed toward a variety of goals. To preserve the integrity of meaning, however, one goal must remain primary. It will serve a foundational purpose in relationship to all of the other goals of Bible study. If we lose sight of or fail to build upon this foundational goal we will not only be violating sound principles of textual interpretation but find ourselves in danger of reading our own ideas into the text rather than discovering the truth which God seeks to convey to us. I refer to this goal as the **primary "A.I.M." of Bible study:**

A: Author's

I: Intended

M: Meaning

In other words, when we affirm that the "meaning" of a text remains constant while its "significance" may vary from person to person, we have still only described our primary goal in part. We want to discover the meaning of the text. But how do we know what the "meaning" is? Who or what determines its "meaning"? What is the "touchstone" by which we determine when we have understood the "meaning" of the text? By what standard can we determine whether our reading of the text is "valid"? The answer to such questions is not as complicated as it might seem at first. The Bible — as an incident of written communication — is not unlike every other act of communication, written or oral, that we engage in everyday. Every day we engage in conversations, write letters, read the newspaper, etc. When we send messages to others — either oral or written — it is because we believe that they are capable of *understanding the message that we intend to convey.* If their response suggests to us that they have interpreted our messages to mean something *other* than what we *intended* them to mean, then we conclude that they have *misunderstood* us. From the perspective of the receiver — whether listener or reader — we trust in the same process. We seek to understand that meaning which the sender *intends* to convey to us. We may misinterpret the message, take it to mean something else. The fault may be with the sender (unclear communication) or with the receiver (not attending closely). Regardless, should we later discover that some other meaning had been *intended* by the sender, we would still consider ourselves to have *misunderstood.*

Faith in this ability to understand sender intent (at least approximately) is inherent in all communicative behavior. It is no less central to the way that we approach our study of the Bible. **If we want to understand the biblical text, we must always ask, "What meaning did the author intend to convey?"** Your personal life experiences may determine the significance of the text for you. But the author's intent is determinative of the text's meaning. It is the only standard by which to sort out the many competing "readings" of any given text. You say the text means this. I say it means that. How can we judge what it *truly* means? Only by measuring our readings against what was — according to our best ability to determine it — the meaning intended by the author can we ascertain whether we have understood the text. Hence, the primary goal of Bible study is not to answer the question, "What does this passage mean to you?" Rather, it is to answer the question, "What meaning did Paul (or Peter, or Luke, or John, etc.) intend to convey?"

THREE PROGRESSIVE OBJECTIVES

Understanding the Author's Intended Meaning (A. I. M.) may be the primary and foundational goal of Bible study but it is not the only goal. Nor are the goals of Bible study limited to "understanding" goals. If we would return to 2 Timothy 3:16-17, we could easily notice that the fourfold "usefulness" of Scripture pertains to goals of "living" and "serving" as well as "understanding." In his first letter, John wrote: "We proclaim to you what we have seen and heard, so that you also may have fellowship with us. And our fellowship is with the Father and with his Son, Jesus Christ" (1 John 1:3, NIV). And so we might speak of "relationship" or "fellowship" (with God) goals as well.

It is important, then, for us to understand that Bible study is an activity which encompasses both the meaning and significance of the text and which addresses not only our understanding of doctrine but the holiness of our lives, the faithfulness of our service and the intimacy of our personal relationship with God. To recognize the foundational role which the author's intended meaning plays, we should always **progress from meaning to significance.** This is the best way to ensure that God's Word will guide our understanding of life experiences and to avoid the pitfall of allowing our life experiences to sit in judgment over the Bible. But as we do so, we should keep in mind that in studying the Bible we should eventually work our way through no less than **three progressive objectives.**

Each of these objectives represents a different stage of understanding, a different benefit gained. Each is also achieved by a different means. By "progressive," I mean that they should be pursued in the sequence suggested for the understanding acquired is cumulative, leading us from meaning to significance. Taken together, however, they constitute a well rounded and balanced set of goals for Bible study. They can be summarized in the following table:

Objective	Understanding	Benefit	Means
"Exposition"	Original Intended Meaning	Historical/Doctrinal Understanding	Five Stages of Analysis
"Interpretation"	Contemporary Significance	Relevance for Present Times	Timeless Principles or Parallel Life Situations
"Application"	Personal Life Relevance	God-Pleasing Life and Faithful Service	Meditation and Reflection; Conviction of the Holy Spirit

The first objective is frequently referred to as **exposition** because its goal is to "expose" or "uncover" the meaning of the text. Since the meaning is determined by the intent of the author, the understanding goal is to recover the original intent of the historical author at the time when the text was written. This is an historical understanding of the particular life situation of the first sender/receivers and the message conveyed at that fixed moment in time — the historical, cultural and situational context of God's revelation. An understanding of the "meaning" of the text provides the basis of our doctrinal understanding ("What does the Bible say about . . .?"). The five principles of exposition which serve as the focus of future lessons represent the means for closing the historical and cultural distance which the reader experiences.

The move from meaning to significance is usually referred to as the art of **interpretation.**[1] "Interpretation" is the act of building a bridge between the word of the past and the world of the present. As such, it seeks to determine the contemporary significance of the historical truth discovered during exposition. Now that we understand what the author "meant," what is the relevance of this truth for life in our present age? There are two primary strategies for discovering the present day relevance of a passage in the Bible.

First, we may search for "timeless principles." What truths are conveyed in the text that, for good reasons, appear to be true apart from the historical circumstances — that would remain true even if the specifics of time, place, and culture would change? In John 13, we read that Jesus washed His disciples' feet and said, "I have set you an example that you should do as I have done for you" (John 13:15). What is the present day relevance of Jesus' example? Should we, too, literally wash each others' feet? Or did Jesus' actions embody a truth or principle that transcends the particular historical circumstances? Certainly, the significance of washing another's feet is different today than it was in the days of Jesus when people traveled in sandal-shod feet over miles of dirty and dusty roads. Perhaps washing the feet of another today would still involve an important lesson in humility and service. But the practical need is significantly different. Perhaps the greater point of relevance is to practice the transcending principle of humility and service in response to the practical needs that people *do* experience today.

In many cases, it may be possible to identify some present day life situation that is sufficiently similar to that of the original life situation so that the specifics of the text *may* be directly applied. In the book of Acts, we read that in the Jerusalem church,

> All the believers were together and had everything in common. Selling their possessions and goods, they gave to anyone as he had need (Acts 2:44-45, NIV).

Many might argue that such a practice is not incumbent upon the church today since (1) a comparison to what Scripture tells us about other congregations demonstrates this to be a voluntary act on the part of the church in Jerusalem rather than a consistent pattern among the New Testament churches and (2) this practice was an act demanded by the circumstances of the time — a level of famine and extreme poverty that required such sharing to provide what was essential for daily survival. These are, in fact, good reasons not to impose such behaviors upon the church today. Yet, should such a life situation present itself to some church today — should its membership become so poor that families could live by no other way — would it be out of the question to suggest that some families ought to demonstrate the love of Christ by sharing what they have with others, even if it means selling some of their possessions?

Ultimately, both "exposition" and "interpretation" should lead us to **application.** Here one seeks to understand not merely the general relevance for people in his own day, but the specific relevance of a passage for his personal life. Here one is motivated not simply by his own desire for understanding but by his desire to please God with his life and to be a faithful servant. Personal life applications will, of course, be found within the "umbrella" of the general relevance of the passage for our times. But only your personal life circumstances can determine the significance of a text for your life. Here there can be no substitute for meditation and reflection. Those who sincerely desire to please God can count on the assistance of the convicting and teaching ministry of His Spirit. This is not to suggest that any kind of special illumination is required for understanding the *meaning* of the text or for arriving at a valid interpretation. Nor is this to suggest that the teaching ministry of the Holy Spirit consists of some new and personal *revelation* to us. But He can guide us by bearing witness within us and through the witness of others as we consider our own personal mix of gifts, passions and opportunities for service.

In the end, it is important to reassert the importance of keeping all three of these progressive objectives in mind. Fruitless Bible study is usually the result of one of two extremes — myopic preoccupations with one end of the process or the other. On one hand, it is possible to become so preoccupied with "exposition" that we never get around to making personal life application. If Bible study does not help me to lead a holy life and be a faithful servant, it becomes a mere academic exercise. On the other hand, we can be in such a hurry to get to personal life application that we neglect to invest the effort to lay the necessary foundation. If personal life application is not grounded in sound exposition and interpretation, we effectively deny the authority and relevancy of God's Word in our lives.

ENDNOTES

1. The more technical term for the art of interpretation is "hermeneutics."

2 BASIC PRINCIPLES OF EXPOSITION

For most new readers the most intimidating and challenging aspect of Bible study is closing the historical and cultural distance between themselves and the biblical text. Skirmishes with Jebusite troops seem far removed from life at the office (or maybe not, depending upon your office). And even though most of us tend to feel a bit more comfortable studying the New Testament, it is still difficult to understand why God would think that questions over whether to eat meat offered to idols might address the needs of twentieth-century Americans. The thought of trying to unravel the mysteries of Revelation — even though most of its imagery consists of "stock" symbols from the Old Testament and first-century culture — is absolutely horrifying.

Because this distance represents the first and biggest challenge for beginners, the remaining lessons in this series will focus on the skills of exposition — that aspect of Bible study which seeks to close that distance and make the meaning of the text accessible for interpretation and application. It is important to remember a key idea conveyed in Lesson One — that fruitful Bible study consists of more than just "Exposition." "Interpretation" and "Application" are also crucial considerations if our Bible study is to be relevant to and have value for the ways we live and serve our God. Nothing to follow should be understood as detracting from their importance. Nevertheless, this is a "first things first" series of lessons. And the first and greatest need that most beginning students have is for training in these basic skills of exposition and for an introduction to some of the tools available to help them enrich their understanding of the biblical text. It will also be helpful to remember that the **five stages of investigation** are not uniquely applicable to the Bible. These stages could be applied in an attempt to understand, more precisely, any written text. Identifying and investigating each of these areas with care, however, has particular value for understanding those texts which require us to close a greater historical and cultural distance. You will simply be learning to apply these stages of investigation to the Bible.

FIVE STAGES OF INVESTIGATING A BIBLE PASSAGE

This lesson will first define the different stages of investigation in the order in which they should be performed and then explain why the order itself is important. The stages of investigation are as follows:

1. SURVEYING THE BACKGROUND

The goal of this first stage of investigation is to recapture the larger historical situation in which the passage was written. This stage, then, seeks to reconstruct the *historical and cultural background* of your text. This stage of investigation will itself be carried on at two levels.

First, this investigation is carried out at the **book** level. You should attempt to ascertain basic facts about the entire work of which your passage is a part. Apply the basic "detective" questions — when? where? who? what? why? how? — to gain insight into the original life situation or the occasion which created a need for your text to be written.

Second, this investigation is carried out at the level of the specific **passage** being studied. What people, places, customs, objects, etc., are mentioned in your passage? What can you find out about them? Investigating background at both of these levels will help you to locate your passage in its own cultural and historical setting.

2. EXAMINING THE CONTEXT

The word "context" literally means "with the text," employing the Latin preposition "con" ("with").[1] In a sense, we could say that the background of the passage is a kind of "context." Each text comes to us with an historical and cultural identity because it was created to address some specific situation at a particular moment in history within a specific culture. Thus we might say that any text has an historical and cultural "context." However, for present purposes, we will reserve this term for the literary context of a passage — the rest of the "text" that comes along with the passage that you are studying. This literary context exists at two levels as well.

First, the reader should consider the **immediate** context of a passage. This would consist, most immediately, of the several verses before and after the "boundaries" you have set for the passage you are studying. It would eventually consist of the paragraph, chapter or book in which your passage is located. What "place" does your passage occupy in the author's scheme? What role does it play in his plan? How does it fit into the "flow" of his argument or explanation?

Your passage will also have a **remote** context. The context eventually consists of any other works in the Bible written by the same author. And since God, in a sense, is the author of all Scripture (the source of its "inspiration"), the ultimate context of every verse is the entire Bible. In other words, we should understand any particular passage in light of what the entire Bible has to say about the same subject and we should also use clear passages to help us understand unclear passages.

3. ANALYZING THE GRAMMAR

In analyzing the grammar of the passage, we attempt to scrutinize its exact wording and pay careful attention to how the writer uses language to construct and convey his meaning. Two considerations can be identified here as well.

First, we should pay attention to the individual **parts of speech** employed. This is perhaps the most laborious and dreaded part of Bible study for many. It's the "nitty-gritty," "down and dirty" part of Bible study. Yet the difference between understanding or misunderstanding the meaning of a passage may very well depend upon whether we understand the difference between how an adjective functions and how an adverb functions — and whether we can identify which one is used in the passage.

Meaning is also constructed by the structure of relationships between ideas and propositions within the passage. Individually, the potential meanings of parts remain ambiguous. Taken together, however, they come to possess coherent meaning for the reader. What is the idea structure of the passage? How do the individual propositions relate to one another? Here sentence flow diagrams are an invaluable aid.

4. DEFINING THE WORDS

Having considered the larger historical and cultural setting of the passage, the literary flow into which the passage fits and the larger structural elements of the passage, the reader should now perform the most minute investigation yet — that of the individual units of meaning, the specific words chosen to convey the author's message. Again, two questions should be pursued.

First, **which words *did* the author employ**? Though we have confidence in the reliability and sufficiency of our English translations we are nonetheless aware that they are translations. The original texts were penned primarily in Hebrew (Old Testament) and Greek (New Testament).[2] You may be surprised to discover that — without learning any Hebrew or Greek — you can learn how to identify the Hebrew or Greek words used in a passage.

But we must also ask **what do these words mean**? What are the different ways in which they can be used? What specific shades of meaning might they convey? In future lessons you will be introduced to tools that will help you to conduct such investigations.

5. CONSULTING THE COMMENTARIES

Commentaries are reference books which contain the verse-by-verse comments upon the text by biblical scholars. Many of these people have specialized in the study of biblical history and biblical languages and bring a great deal of professional expertise to the text — far more than the average person. We should be anxious to learn from them. Their comments contain the fruit of their own investigations into background, context, grammar and words. Nevertheless, we want to read them critically. The fact that even the "specialists" disagree at times should warn us never to simply take someone else's word about what the Bible means. We can and should learn from others but a commitment to our own spiritual growth always places upon us the responsibility for a firsthand experience with God's Word.

THE ORDER OF INVESTIGATION

This *order* for the stages of investigation has significance as well. There are two reasons for performing the stages in the order presented.

First, this order enables the reader to move from the general to the particular. Picturing the stages of investigation as a series of concentric circles may help to depict the relationship between the stages:

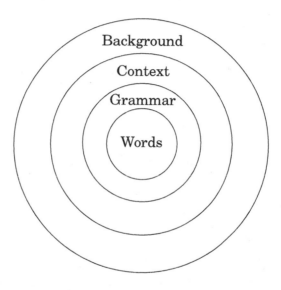

Background investigation first places the passage within the broadest of its settings, locating its time and place within the flow of human history and diversity of human cultures. Examining the context places the passage within narrower settings — the flow of Scripture itself as well as the flow of the particular work of which the passage is a part. Analyzing the grammar begins to narrow the focus to the structure of the passage itself. Defining the words focuses on how the individual units take on meaning in the context of these larger structures. Taken together and in this order, the five stages of investigation constitute a process which becomes ever more particular in its focus, gradually narrowing the object of investigation so that each succeeding stage can be conducted in light of previous discoveries. Consulting commentaries, of course, will bring us back to the "big picture" as the commentaries add to our knowledge of all areas of investigation — background, context, grammar and words. The final stage of investigation, then, draws us back outside of our own firsthand work and encourages a synthesis of our various observations into a coherent understanding of the text. Thus our diagram might be completed this way:

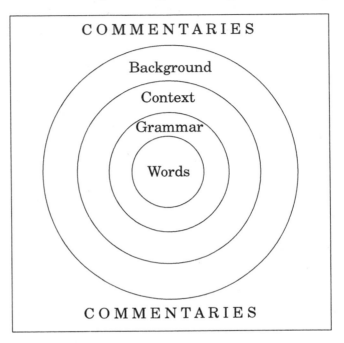

A second reason for respecting this order of investigation is to protect our ability to read the commentaries critically. By conducting the stages in this order we develop a firsthand acquaintance with the text before we consult the opinions of others. Since many of the tools you will use to conduct the stages of investigation are "secondary" sources (i.e., they still represent the fruits of someone else's study) it is not quite accurate to say that the distinction here is between "primary" and "secondary" sources. The Bible, however, is our chief "primary" source and by conducting these stages of investigation it is fair to say that we have begun to experience the text ourselves rather than letting someone else deliver a prepackaged interpretation for our acceptance. It is also worth remembering that something is not true just because it appears in print. The publishing house of the Jehovah's Witnesses — the Watchtower Bible and Tract Society — is among the largest religious publishers in the world. This does not mean that they publish truth. It is important for us to have some firsthand work with the text "under our belts" before we go to the commentaries so that we can evaluate what we read. Reading commentaries before we begin our own investigation can create "blindspots" on our part as we find it difficult to shake the biases that we may have formed as a result of reading the commentary.

ENDNOTES

1. T. Norton Sterrett, *Understanding Your Bible* (Downers Grove, IL: InterVarsity Press, 1978), p. 49.

2. Small portions of the Old Testament (Genesis 31:47; Jeremiah 10:11; Ezra 4:8–6:18; 7:12-26; Daniel 2:4b–7:28) actually come to us in Aramaic, a "sister" language of Hebrew.

3 CHOOSING A BIBLE AND A TEXT

Tools	Skills
Various Versions of the English Bible	*Selecting a Bible to read*
Parallel Bibles	*Comparing English Versions*
Various Editions of Study Bibles	*Choosing a text to study*

Even before the reader begins the first stage of investigation, she must make choices that will effect her Bible study significantly. A text will be chosen for study. A particular version or versions of the Bible will be chosen from which to study. The reader may even choose to use one of the many "Study Bibles" (an edition of the Bible which contains a variety of study aids — introductions, footnotes, maps, a concordance, etc.) currently on the market. All of these decisions will precede the first stage of investigation. For this reason, our consideration of tools and skills will begin with a discussion of these important choices.

The goal of this lesson is not to create dissatisfaction with whatever Bible you may have already purchased or with a Bible which has been in your family for years. Generally speaking, almost all of our modern translations are sufficient for one purpose or another. Also, no single translation stands out clearly as the only or obviously best choice for all the stages of investigation. For this reason, there is no inherent problem with choosing any of the modern English translations for one's primary reference text and, at some points of our investigation, we will want to compare more than one translation regardless of our choice of a primary text. For those who may feel a strong loyalty to the King James tradition, it is worth noting that, even though it is much older than the other major English versions, it still falls within the broad boundaries of "modern."

As a result, if you have developed a preference for a particular version of the Bible, you need not abandon it. Nor should we ever encourage the development of overly rigid and narrow attitudes about which is the "right" version of the Bible, compared to which all other versions are "wrong." Nevertheless the choice of a Bible should be made carefully, for several reasons. First, each of the different translations has its own set of strengths and weaknesses. Each thus offers its own set of benefits and suffers from its own set of limitations. As a result, it is not always easy to make a decision in favor of one translation over others. In addition, once we choose a Bible and become familiar with it, most of us tend to develop a "comfortable feeling" about it. We get used to the way it reads and to the format of its pages. Sometimes we can even visualize the way certain passages appear on the page and this helps us to remember where to find them. Handwritten notes accumulate in the margins. Unless you neglect it, this Bible will soon become a familiar friend and adjusting to a new and different Bible will become increasingly difficult. Second, some versions will serve well for devotional reading but not necessarily for the kinds of investigation that we will learn to perform. This issue will be discussed in more detail a bit later. Finally, many see the different "Study Bibles" as attractive choices because of the "study helps" they contain. Yet there are advantages and disadvantages to the use of such a "Study Bible" and the various editions themselves are not all of equal quality. For all of these reasons, we should consider carefully which Bible(s) we will use for our study.

CHOOSING A BIBLE

CHOOSING THE VERSION(S)

As we consider the various English versions, we must keep two important distinctions in mind. These distinctions will help us to understand some of the differences between the versions.

The first distinction is that between the **translation** and the **paraphrase**. Some English versions represent "translations," others represent "paraphrases." These categories of versions differ in two important ways.

First, they differ in their primary sources. A "translation" works primarily from the original Greek and Hebrew manuscripts. That is, it is an attempt to take a statement made in one language (Greek or Hebrew) and put it into a statement in a different language (English) which conveys the same meaning. A "paraphrase" does not work primarily from the original language manuscripts but from another English version. That is, it is an attempt to take a statement made in one language (English) and to put it into a different statement in the same language (still English) which conveys the same meaning.[1] Thus we might say that while *The Living Bible* is a paraphrase (since the primary source of Kenneth Taylor's version was another English version — the *American Standard Version* of 1901[2]) the *New American Standard Version* is a translation (since, although it sought to preserve "the lasting values of the ASV," its primary textual basis was Kittel's latest edition of *Biblia Hebraica* and the 23rd edition of the Nestle-Aland Greek New Testament[3]). The former mainly produced a restatement of another English version while the latter actually produced a fresh rendering of the original languages into English.

Translations and paraphrases also differ in their goals. A translation seeks to "retain the formal details as far as possible, and still carry the message with the spirit of the passage preserved and an impact on the reader similar to that intended by the original author."[4] The paraphrase is often difficult to identify with the saying in the original because its goal is not simply to *translate* but to *explain* the text. Hence, a paraphrase will often read quite differently than any of the major translations. Whereas 1 Kings 20:11 is translated "Let not him who girds on his armor boast like him who takes it off" in the *New American Standard,* it is translated "Don't count your chickens before they hatch!" in *The Living Bible.* Also, a paraphrase will often add to the text explanations which are not implicit in the text itself — "expanding where necessary for a clear understanding by the modern reader."[5] The paraphraser is not necessarily unaware of the risks here:

> There are dangers in paraphrases, as well as values. For whenever an author's exact words are not translated from the original languages, there is a possibility that the translator, however honest, may be giving the English reader something that the original writer did not mean to say. This is because a paraphrase is guided not

only by the translator's skill in simplifying but also by the clarity of his understanding of what the author meant and by his theology.[6]

1 Peter 3:21 ("In baptism we show that we have been saved from death," *The Living Bible*; "baptism now saves you," *New American Standard*) and Romans 4:12 ("for Abraham found favor with God by faith alone," *The Living Bible*; "the faith of our father Abraham which he had while uncircumcised," *New American Standard*) are just a couple of examples of such interpretive expansions. Lewis Foster puts it well when he notes that a paraphrase "is more like a minister's sermon about the Bible and not the Bible itself."[7]

In addition to the distinction between translations and paraphrases, it might also be helpful to distinguish between two different categories of translations: **form-literal** translations and **dynamic** translations. The basis of this distinction consists of the degree to which the translation attempts to literally reproduce, in the English translation, the surface structures (i.e., the grammatical forms, the number and order of words, etc.) of the Greek and Hebrew texts.

Generally speaking, there are two different schools of thought as to whether the literal reproduction of form is a positive or negative quality in a translation. Most translators agree that the most important goal of a translation is to communicate the meaning of the original. Some believe that the meaning of the original is best communicated when the translation imitates, as closely as possible, the formal or structural features of the original language. Others, however, believe that the meaning of the original is best communicated when translated into natural forms of the "receptor" language,[8] whether this imitates the form of the original language or not.[9] The former school of thought holds that to reproduce the form *is* to reproduce the meaning. The latter holds that it is often necessary to *change* the form in order to reproduce the same meaning in a new and different language. Those translations, then, which apply a "formal correspondence" philosophy (such as the *American Standard* and later the *New American Standard*) will stay as close to the original form as possible — at times even opting for English expressions which are complex and awkward in order to imitate the number and order of the forms in the original, word for word. Those translations which opt for "dynamic equivalency" (such as the *Good News Bible*), on the other hand, will prefer natural English forms — even when these do not closely parallel the original forms — in order to "stimulate in the new reader essentially the same reaction to the text as the original author wished to produce in his first and immediate hearers."[10]

Few of our modern translations are exclusively form-literal or dynamic in their renderings. The difference, then, is usually one of degree — each different version may be visualized as a different point on a continuum between an extreme commitment to form literalness and an extreme commitment to dynamic equivalency, as in the following diagram which is probably representative of the broad characteristics of a few versions:

Form-Literal   Dynamic
—X———————X————————————X——————————X—
American   Revised   New International   Good News
Standard   Standard   Version

Understanding the difference between the "form-literal" and the "dynamic equivalency" approaches not only helps to explain why we have different versions and why they are worded differently, but why different versions may be useful for different purposes — as will become evident in subsequent lessons.

To assist you in assessing the relative strengths and weaknesses of the various major translations, **A Survey of Bible Translations** is included at the end of this lesson. It will examine (in chronological order) the most popular versions. If you have further questions, you would do well to consult a minister or elder in your local church. It is also possible to purchase a **Parallel Bible** which will include several different English versions in parallel columns so that the reader can compare different translations. **The New Layman's Parallel Bible**, published by Zondervan, includes the *King James*, the *New International, The Living Bible* and the *Revised Standard* versions. **The Comparative Study Bible**, also published by Zondervan, includes the *New International*, the *New American Standard*, the *King James* and the *Amplified* versions. There is an advantage to having several different versions open for examination at one time in a single volume. However, due to the volume of material, most Parallel Bibles are bulky and not very portable.

USING "STUDY BIBLES"

Deciding which version(s) to use is only one consideration in choosing a Bible. There is also a great host of "study editions" available to the Bible student. The choices are multiplied by the fact that many of these "Study Bibles" are also available in more than one version. The goal of the "Study Bible" is to package various study "helps" along with the biblical text in a single volume. As mentioned above, these helps may take on various forms — introductions to each book of the Bible, explanatory footnotes at the bottoms of the pages, lists of "cross-reference" verses in the margins, concordances or maps in a separate section at the end of the Bible, etc. As such they are an attractive alternative for the new student looking to choose a new Bible.

There are both benefits and risks to using a Study Bible, however. The main benefit is that it can serve as a relatively inexpensive and portable reference library. While the selection of "helps" will vary from edition to edition, these tools have value for each of the different stages of investigation. The introductions and footnotes can provide helpful background information, the outlines can help us to consider immediate context, the cross-reference passages can help us to examine remote context, the concordance can be helpful for locating key passages and many of the notes and articles provide commentary. The **NIV Study Bible**, published by Zondervan, is an example of a study edition which includes a comparatively extensive set of such helps.

There are risks, however. Perhaps the most significant risk is that of substituting the interpretations offered by the notes for our firsthand work with the text. You might remember that, in the previous lesson, a case was made for reserving commentary research for the end of your investigation. When explanatory footnotes are so immediately available — right at the bottom of the same page of our Bibles — it is easy to consult them without performing our own investigation first and thus develop biases toward the text. It can also be easy to forget that these notes are *not* the Bible but *about* the Bible, since they are right there *in* the Bible. The Scriptures are inspired

— the footnotes are not! Also, we should keep in mind that while these helps offer us additional information with which to understand the text, they often provide a minimal amount of that information. Many of the tools which you will learn to use in the lessons ahead will provide you with more and sometimes better information. Depending solely upon the "helps" in the Study Bible can often cause us to become lazy, substituting partial and superficial study for a more complete and honest investigation.

After considering the benefits and risks of using a Study Bible, you may want to at least acquire one Bible that contains paragraph divisions and a list of cross-reference verses. These two features will be particularly helpful for reasons to be discussed later.

CHOOSING A PASSAGE TO STUDY

As difficult as it may be for some people to settle on their choice of a Bible, many will find the choice of a passage to study the most difficult of all. After all, having a Bible is one matter. Deciding which of the 31,100 verses to study is another. You might find these six suggestions helpful:

1. Study systematically through larger portions of Scripture (books, chapters, etc.), bit by bit, paragraph by paragraph.

2. Study passages which you have difficulty understanding — maybe the words themselves are not clear to you or else you have trouble understanding the teaching (or "doctrine") of the passage.

3. Study passages which appear to be theologically significant — passages that touch on the "big themes" of the Bible — God, Christ, Salvation, etc.

4. Study passages which are controversial — passages which people tend to interpret differently. This may be especially helpful for responding to the questions of people to whom you are trying to witness.

5. Study passages which seem to relate to some aspect of your personal life situation.

6. Study passages that you notice and mark during times of devotional reading, when you are not yet attempting to do "close study."

A SURVEY OF
MAJOR BIBLE TRANSLATIONS

King James Version. Translated in 1611 by a team of translators, appointed by King James, who performed their work in the context of the Church of England and Puritan theology. The manuscripts upon which this translation was based are not as ancient or reliable as those upon which more recent translations are based. Primarily form-literal, the accuracy is nonetheless good. Its Elizabethan English still makes for eloquence in public reading and thus has a tremendous aesthetic appeal for many. This is also its greatest weakness, however, for three centuries of evolution within the English language have rendered many of its terms obsolete. (See 2 Thessalonians 2:7; 1 Thessalonians 4:15; Acts 28:13 for examples.)

American Standard Version. Appeared in 1901 as an American edition of a British project to revise the *King James Version.* Produced by a commitee representing nine American Protestant denominations. Sought to take advantage of the more ancient and more reliable Greek manuscripts discovered since the translation of the *KJV.* Aimed to be as form-literal as possible and to make the Bible more readable to Americans. Much of its language will still be found to be obsolete and difficult to understand by present day readers, however.

Revised Standard Version. A later revision of the *American Standard Version,* the New Testament appeared in 1946 and the Old Testament in 1952. Attempted to employ more current English while staying as close to the King James tradition as possible. Translated under the auspices of the National Council of Churches. Restores some of the eloquence of the *KJV* but is also clearer and less form-literal than either the *KJV* or the *ASV.*

New American Standard Bible. New Testament appeared in 1963, the Old Testament in 1970. Produced by fifty-eight anonymous scholars under the sponsorship of the Lockman Foundation. Reflects an evangelical theological background. Somewhat based on the *ASV* but primarily a fresh translation. Like the *ASV,* strongly form-literal. This makes it good for grammar study but it is often difficult to understand because the English is awkward at times.

Good News Bible (Today's English Version). New Testament appeared in 1966, the Old Testament in 1976. Produced by Robert Bratcher (Southern Baptist) and the American Bible Society. The first true "dynamic equivalence" translation, it seeks to put the Bible into common, everyday English and is aimed at the elementary school reading level. Includes introductions to and outlines of each Bible book. Text is illustrated with line drawings. Based on the best Greek and Hebrew texts now available. Accuracy is really very good although some of its renderings have been controversial and closer to free paraphrase. Its clarity and readability make it good for devotional reading or for the beginning Bible reader but less helpful for close grammar study.

The Living Bible. First appeared complete in 1971. A paraphrase rather than a translation. Prepared by Kenneth Taylor who depended primarily upon the 1901 *American Standard Version.* Taylor's theological background is evangelical but his paraphrase is at times influenced by his personal theological slant and is expanded for commentary. As a paraphrase, its readability is excellent, but accuracy often suffers. Not a good basis for serious Bible study.

New International Version. New Testament appeared in 1973, Old Testament in 1978. Produced by over one hundred scholars representing various denominations under the sponsorship of the New York International Bible Society. Its background is solidly evangelical, although it evidences a strong influence by Reformed theology in places. Like the *Good News Bible,* based upon the best Greek and Hebrew manuscripts now available. Though not a true "dynamic," translation it is definitely a "free" translation (i.e., not bound to the form-literal approach). Both accuracy and clarity are good. First English version to rival the King James in popularity.

New King James Version. New Testament appeared in 1979, Old Testament in 1982. A fresh revision of the *KJV* (ignoring the *ASV* and *RSV*) produced by 130 evangelical scholars and sponsored by Thomas Nelson publishers. Seeks to protect the language of the *KJV* while making obsolete passages clear through the use of modern grammar (i.e., substituting current forms of pronouns for "thee," "thou," "thine," etc.). Ignores best Greek manuscripts now available for an 1881 manuscript in order to remain faithful to the King James tradition. Claims to follow the form-literal approach of *KJV* but uses dynamic equivalence and even paraphrase in places.

New Revised Standard Version. Appeared complete in 1990. Further revision of the line of translations dating back to *RSV, ASV,* and *KJV.* Produced by a committee composed of both men and women from Protestant, Roman Catholic, Eastern Orthodox and Jewish groups. Authorized and endorsed by the National Council of Churches. Gives special attention to use of non-gender-oriented language.

SOURCES

Foster, Lewis. *Selecting a Translation of the Bible.* Cincinnati: Standard Publishing, 1978.
Lewis, Jack P. *The English Bible from KJV to NIV: A History and Evaluation.* 2nd ed. Grand Rapids: Baker, 1991.

ENDNOTES

1. John Beekman and John Callow, *Translating the Word of God* (Grand Rapids: Zondervan, 1974), p. 21*n*.

2. Kenneth Taylor, interview in "The Story of 'The Living Bible,'" *Eternity* 23 (April 1973), p. 74.

3. Preface, *New American Standard Bible*, p. viii-ix.

4. Lewis Foster, *Selecting a Translation of the Bible* (Cincinnati: Standard Publishing, 1978), p. 41.

5. Preface to *The Living Bible.*

6. *Ibid.*

7. Lewis Foster, *Selecting a Translation of the Bible*, p. 41.

8. That is, the language into which the translation is made.

9. Beekman and Callow, *Translating the Word of God*, p. 20.

10. Eugene Nida, *Good News for Everyone* (Waco: Word Books, 1977), p. 13.

4 SURVEYING THE BACKGROUND

Tools	Skills
Bible Dictionaries	*Reconstructing Life Situations*
Bible Encyclopedias	*Determining Occasion and Purpose*
Bible Atlases	*Understanding Specific References*
	to Persons, Places, Objects and Customs

As we begin our approach to the passage we have chosen to study, we find ourselves in a foreign land. Thanks to the diligent work of our translators, we have the text in our language. But the times, the places, the people, and the customs are not those of our own daily world. Broadly defined, this intersection of time, place, people and custom is what we mean by the term **culture**. Bible study is thus an **intercultural** experience and most of us find ourselves culturally disadvantaged in the world of the Bible.

This first stage of investigation attempts to close the historical and cultural distance between the text and the reader by locating the passage within its original setting — the life situation of the author and his immediate audience. Reconstructing this life situation requires that we treat our passage as an act of communication. Every act of communication originates in a sender, is addressed to a receiver and is mediated through some vehicle.

Ultimately, of course, God is the sender of the message of the Bible. Considered at this level, the message of the Bible is addressed to all people, in all cultures, for all time. As a result, *we* can say that the Bible is God's word to *us*. But the vehicle — the Bible — was also produced through the minds, hearts and hands of the men whom God inspired. Peter observed that "prophecy never had its origin in the will of man, but men spoke from God as they were carried along by the Holy Spirit" (2 Peter 1:21, NIV). While Peter emphasized the ultimate inspired source of the message, he nevertheless recognized the agency of the human sender as well. Though God's message to us transcends the limits of time and culture, that message is communicated to us through a vehicle which is local to a particular time and culture. Each part of the Bible was written *at* a particular time, *by* particular people *in* particular places, *to* particular people *in* particular places, and *for* particular reasons. God's revelation is thus an *historical* revelation. He has chosen to communicate a timeless message through an instrument created within and bearing the marks of human history and culture. This is the accommodation of an infinite and transcendent Sender to finite receivers whose potential to understand is fixed by the limits of time and space.

The practical result is that our Bible study must respect the need to consider the message of the Bible in its historical and cultural setting. To discover "what the Bible mean*s*" we must discover "what the Bible mean*t*." To do this, we must treat our passage as an *historical* act of communication, doing our best to reconstruct the original life situation of the senders and receivers and to understand the form and contents of the vehicle (the text). In pursuit of our major **A.I.M.** (Author's Intended Meaning), then, the specific **goals** of "Surveying the Background" can be summarized as follows:

1. To reconstruct the original life situation of both the author and target audience.
2. To understand the historical and cultural significance of specific references within the text.
3. To "receive" the text in a manner as much like the original audience as possible.

Achieving the first two goals should enable us to achieve the third. As a result, investigating the background of the passage can be divided into two phases: reconstructing the **specific historical situation** which created the need for the text to be written and exploring the **larger cultural background** to help us discover the significance of references made within the passage.

RECONSTRUCTING THE SPECIFIC HISTORICAL SITUATION

In this phase, we want to gather information about the sender, receiver(s) and vehicle. Specifically, we should attempt to answer, to the best of our ability, the following questions. These questions will apply to the entire work of which the passage is a part, rather than directly to the passage itself. They are more specific than questions we will ask later in the sense that they apply to a specific situation rather than to ongoing cultural conditions.

A) Who was the **author** of the text? What else does the Bible tell us about him?

B) What was the **place of origin** for the text? Why was the author there? What was happening there?

C) Who were the **recipients** of the text? For whom was it intended? Where did they live? What was happening there?

D) What was the **date** of the text? What was happening in the lives of the sender(s) and receiver(s) at this time?

E) What was the **occasion** of the text? For what purpose was it written? What problem was it designed to solve? What need was it designed to meet? What questions was it designed to answer?

F) What is the **"genre"**[1] of the text? In what style was it written? Which literary form was employed? What were the expected features of such a literary form?

EXPLORING THE LARGER CULTURAL BACKGROUND

In this second phase, we should focus on references made within the passage itself. Though we narrow our attention from the work as a whole to the specific passage being studied, the questions we need to ask now are really broader than those asked earlier since they take us beyond the immediate circumstances surrounding the passage to larger cultural conditions and ongoing customs and institutions. Taken together, however, the answers to both sets of questions help us to understand the historical/cultural background both generally and specifically. Appropriate questions to apply to the passage itself are as follows:

A) What **people** are mentioned in the passage? Are any **individual persons** named? For example, what do we know about "King Agrippa" mentioned in Acts 25:13? Are any **groups** of people named? For example, why might it be significant that the question of Matthew 22:23 was posed by the "Sadducees"? What do we know about them?

B) What **places** are mentioned in the passage? Where were these places? What significant events occurred there? Why were they significant at the time of writing? Do they possess any religious, political or geographical significance? For example, is there any possible significance to the fact that Jesus asked his disciples, "Who do people say the Son of Man is?" while He was in "the region of Caesarea Philippi" (Matthew 16:13)?

C) Does the passage refer to any **physical objects** which may have had any particular significance? For example, when Jesus told the parable about the lost son, of what significance were the robe, ring and sandals given to the son upon his return (Luke 15:22)?

D) Do any of the **customs** or **practices** mentioned in the text seem to have particular historical or cultural significance? For example, what was the significance of a woman not wearing a head covering in public (1 Corinthians 11:5-6)?

TOOLS TO USE

At this point, you may be wondering where you can possibly find such information. Several tools are available to assist us in both phases of this investigation. These tools can be divided into three classes.

One class is the **Bible Dictionary**. This is generally a single volume reference tool. It consists mainly of brief articles, alphabetically arranged, containing a synthesis of data contained in the Bible and other historical sources. A good Bible dictionary can serve as a portable and relatively affordable source of background information. **The New International**

Dictionary of the Bible, published by Zondervan, and **The New Bible Dictionary (2nd edition)**, published by InterVarsity Press, are helpful resources. The best procedure is to look up the article on the Bible book which contains your passage ("Genesis," "Colossians," etc.) and read for specific situational background. From this article, you may get ideas about other articles to look up for information on the city ("Colosse"), the literary genre ("Epistle"), other people ("Epaphras"), etc. Finally, you can look up articles on specific references made in your passage (compare the examples above under "Exploring Larger Cultural Background").

Another class is the **Bible Encyclopedia**. The procedure for using a Bible encyclopedia is identical to that for using a Bible dictionary. The difference is that a Bible encyclopedia will usually be a multi-volume work. The advantage to using a Bible encyclopedia is that it will contain more information — it will include a greater number of articles and will treat topics more extensively. A Bible encyclopedia, however, is less portable and more expensive. **The Zondervan Pictorial Bible Encyclopedia** (5 volumes) is a useful resource. **The International Standard Bible Encyclopedia, Revised** (4 volumes), published by Eerdmans, is an excellent and more recent work. Be sure to consult the new revised edition, edited by Geoffrey Bromiley, rather than the older edition, edited by James Orr.

A good **Bible Atlas** can also provide helpful historical and geographical information. It will usually contain better maps than those found in the dictionaries and encyclopedias and more information from archaeological sources. For these reasons, a Bible atlas can be a helpful supplement to a good Bible dictionary or encyclopedia. The best procedure for using a Bible atlas is to use the indexes in the back of the atlas. The **Zondervan NIV Atlas of the Bible** includes not only maps and articles but a chronological chart of Bible history, a glossary and index of cities/geographical areas, a Scripture index and an index of persons. **The New Bible Atlas**, published by InterVarsity Press, is also an excellent tool.

ENDNOTES

1. More extensive discussions of the role of *genre* in reading Scripture can be found in *How to Read the Bible for All Its Worth* by Gordon Fee and Douglas Stuart (Zondervan, 2nd ed., 1993) and in *How to Read the Bible As Literature . . . And Get More Out of It* by Leland Ryken (Zondervan, 1984).

COMPLETE THE EXERCISE
FOR LESSON FOUR

In addition to knowing the purpose and use of the recommended tools, it is important to gain firsthand experience applying them to the study of a passage. One of the goals of this series of lessons is for you to *learn* Bible study by *doing* Bible study. As a result, each lesson is followed by an exercise — one for each stage of investigation — designed to guide you through the study of a passage of Scripture. To complete the exercises, you will need to consult some of the tools mentioned in this chapter. It is never a poor idea to purchase some of these tools and to build a good library for home Bible study. Another possibility is to suggest that copies of the suggested tools be purchased and added to your church library. If you cannot gain access to these particular tools, you might try completing the exercises with similar tools of the same type produced by other authors/publishers.

The same passage will be the focus of all exercises: Colossians 1:15-20. This is necessary to model the application of all the various stages of investigation in the study of a single passage. Keep in mind that, in the case of any given passage, not all stages are likely to yield great treasures of new insight. In most cases, some stages will be found more helpful than others. Which stages will be found most helpful will be determined by what there is to discover in and about the passage. For one passage, a certain piece of background information may prove very suggestive regarding the meaning of the passage while the grammar analysis fails to reveal much of significance. For another passage, there may be few references in the text that are understood more clearly in historical context, yet a word study may prove enlightening. However, since the student of the Bible is unable to know beforehand what he will discover at each stage, the careful student will be disciplined in completing all stages of investigation into each passage studied. We never know what there is to find — until we look. Some of the important information to be noted in each exercise is contained in Appendix Two at the end of this book so that either (1) a teacher or group leader can discuss your exercise with you or (2) you can check your own work.

LESSON FOUR EXERCISE: SURVEYING THE BACKGROUND

Sample Study: Colossians 1:15-20

1. Look up the article on "Colossians" in *The New International Dictionary of the Bible* (p. 227) and find the answers to the following questions.

   a. When did Paul write this letter and what was his situation at the time?

   b. What was Paul's relationship to the church in Colosse?

   c. Who helped to start the church in Colosse and who were some of the other members there when this letter was written?

d. Why did Paul write a letter to this church? Describe the problem there.

2. From the above article, we learned that "Colosse" was the name of the city where the "Colossians" lived. Now use the article on "Colosse" (p. 227) to answer the following questions:

a. How did the city get its name?

b. Describe the importance of the city.

3. Use the location index in the back of *The NIV Bible Atlas* to find "Colosse" (p. 231). Locate "Colosse" on the map of 1st and 2nd century churches (p. 187).

a. List some of the cities near Colosse.

b. Compare the map on p. 186. In what Roman province was Colosse?

c. When was Colosse considered a "significant Christian community"?

4. In *The New International Dictionary of the Bible,* it is suggested that the false teaching at Colosse may have been "incipient Gnosticism" (p. 227). Look up the article on "Gnosticism" (p. 393) and list some of its basic teachings:

5. It also indicated that "Colossians" was a letter. Look up the article on "epistle" (p. 319). What does this suggest about the possible purpose of "Colossians"?

6. Read Colossians 1:15-20. List some of the statements made in the text that may take on new significance in light of the specific historical situation:

7. Look up the article on "Firstborn" in *The New International Dictionary of the Bible* (p. 353).

   a. What special privileges did the firstborn son of an Israelite possess? How might these privileges apply to Jesus?

   b. Who is referred to as the firstborn of God in the Old Testament (Psalm 89:27)?

8. Look up the article on "Cross" in *The New International Dictionary of the Bible* (p. 241). As you read the description of the act of crucifixion, what stands out to you?

9. Summarize the most important fruits of your survey of the background:

5 EXAMINING THE CONTEXT

Tools	Skills
Outlines of Books of the Bible	*Identifying the Theme and Plan*
A Bible with:	*of Book and Passage*
Cross-Reference System	*Identifying Connecting Words*
Paragraph Divisions	*Using Clear Passages to Interpret*
Topical Bibles	*Unclear Passages*

Having placed the passage within its historical setting — time, place, situation, and culture — you are now ready to proceed with the next stage of investigation: placing the passage within the "flow" of **literary context**.

The word "context" literally means "with" (Latin preposition, *con*) the "text." Interpreting a passage "in context," then, means that we seek to understand how our passage relates to the rest of the "text" that surrounds it. *Reading passages in their context is absolutely essential for understanding the **author's intended meaning**!* Numerous and famous examples testify to the importance of context for communication. We regularly hear of celebrities, star athletes, and politicians who claim to have been misrepresented by the media or by their opponents because statements which they made were repeated "out of context." That is, sentences (or sometimes even fragments of sentences) which they have uttered have been restated, printed, or broadcast in isolation from the other sentences which surrounded those statements. The result is that readers and listeners understand those statements to mean something *other than what the speaker intended*. The receiver is led into *mis*understanding because some other party has separated the sender's statement from its context and the receiver no longer has the benefit of the "surrounding" material to aid their understanding. Even if you can't remember any examples, you may remember a time when you have been the victim of such distortion.

The Bible, as an act of communication, is subject to the same type of distortion when its passages are taken out of context. Are Bible passages ever interpreted out of context in the church? Unfortunately, yes. Most of us probably do it at one time or another even though we may try very hard to avoid it. This does not mean that it is an acceptable practice. It does mean that we need to be on constant guard against it. Even common practices which are beneficial for other purposes can encourage us to ignore context. Memory verses are often learned by rote in isolation from their context. Various Bible indexes, including concordances and topical Bibles (the use of which we will examine in due course), can be helpful for locating key verses in the Bible but they print phrases and verses in isolation from their context. "Chronological" or "Narrative" Bibles which seek to reorder biblical material in historical sequence (i.e., inserting epistles from Paul throughout the book of Acts or harmonizing the four Gospels) can help us to see the sequential relationship between events in the Bible. However, this practice tends to violate both the literary unity of the inspired texts and the integrity of the inspired author's plan in developing his work. The *flow* of *literary* context becomes muddled. The principle of context may seem simple and obvious. But it is also easy to violate this principle unless the student of Scripture is firmly committed to examining the context of the passage under investigation.

TWO LEVELS OF CONTEXT

You might remember from Lesson Two that there are two levels of context which must be investigated. The **immediate** context consists of that provided by the "book" (i.e., the letter, gospel, etc.) of which the passage is a part. *Most* immediately, it will consist of the verses which you find directly preceding and following the "boundaries" you have set for the passage to be studied. From this point, the context gradually expands into ever widening blocks of material — paragraphs, chapters, sections, etc. — as you place your "unit" within the flow of the author's argument or explanation and eventually into the overall plan of the entire book.

Remote context refers to the relationship between the passage being studied and the rest of the Bible. Though each "book" of the Bible is a unified work within itself, it is also a part of that single larger book, the "Bible." The Bible is more than just a collection of sixty-six independent essays. It is an integrated and unified work with a single heart and center — the saving work of God in Jesus Christ. It is consistent in its theology and in its revelation of a single plan of redemption. We must always remember that there is ultimately a single author of Scripture for the same God inspired its several human authors. As a result, the eventual context of every verse of the Bible is the entire Bible. Not only can we examine other works in the Bible by the same author for relevant contextual information, we have an obligation to understand any particular passage in light of what the entire Bible has to say on relevant subjects. This will not only help us to *test* our understanding of the passage in light of other Scripture but enable us to use *clear* passages to help us understand *unclear* passages. These are the values of examining remote context.

EXAMINING THE IMMEDIATE CONTEXT

Because the immediate context is readily at hand and most likely to affect your first reading of the passage, it is perhaps both best and easiest to begin your investigation at this level. Remember that the goal at this point is to grasp how the passage "fits" into the theme and plan of the book and how its meaning is affected by the "flow" of material surrounding it.

READ THE ENTIRE WORK IN A SINGLE SITTING

The first step may be the most challenging for some. *It is important to begin the investigation of immediate context by reading the entire work in a single sitting.* This may be less of a challenge if you wish to study a passage in James. It will be more of a challenge if you wish to study a passage in Isaiah. While you may retain few microscopic details from this reading, it is important for you to gain an initial impression of the work *as a whole* and to experience the *flow* of the work *without interruption.* Let's not kid ourselves — good Bible study demands hard work. Devote an evening to this project. There is little of redemptive worth on television anyway. Keep a small notepad

handy and don't be afraid to mark in your Bible. Remember that
the devil is not afraid of a clean Bible! As you read, look for:

- any clear statement of purpose or any clear statement
  of a problem that the book is intended to solve (good
  examples are John 20:20, 31; Galatians 1:6; 1 John
  5:13; and 1 Timothy 1:3-5).
- repeated words or subjects which may provide clues to
  the key theme(s) of the book (when reading through
  Ephesians, for example, one would want to note the repetition in 1:9, 10; 2:14-22; 4:4-6, 13).

MAKE OR READ AN OUTLINE AND THEME SENTENCE

The second step is designed to bring your initial impressions
into sharper focus: *make or read an outline and theme sentence
for the book.* It is best to do as much of your own work as possible. Skim through your notes and back over the pages of your
Bible. Try to identify, to the best of your ability, the major tran-
sitions in the book — break it down into its main sections or
divisions. Try to paraphrase the central idea of the book in your
own words, in a single sentence. After you have prepared your
own rough draft, you might find it helpful to compare outlines
prepared by others and to make adjustments. Prepared outlines
can be found in many of the study editions of the Bible as well
as in the Bible Dictionary and Bible Encyclopedia articles on
the book. If you feel intimidated or inadequate at the thought of
outlining the book yourself, don't be discouraged. Use the outlines provided in the tools. While it is best to prefer firsthand
experience with the Bible whenever possible, it is far better to
consult a prepared outline and get some idea of the plan of the
book than it is to ignore this level of context altogether.

LOCATE THE PASSAGE

Third, *locate the passage within the plan of the book.* What
does it contribute to the theme? In what section is it located? If
your passage consists of a paragraph (paragraphs frequently
make for good units of study), how does the preceding paragraph "prepare" for it and how does it, in turn, prepare for the
following paragraph? If your passage is smaller than a paragraph, how does it fit into the theme of the paragraph? Keep in
mind that the editors of our Bibles often provide us with infor-

mation that is suggestive for reading our passage in the "flow" of context. Paragraph divisions, chapter and verse divisions and section headings can be helpful at times. However, you should also remember that these *are* editorial additions to the text of the Bible and thus are not infallible. For example, many Bibles place an editorial section heading between verses 21 and 22 of Ephesians 5. The heading creates the impression that there is a major break or transition at this point in the text when, in fact, the verb "submit" in verse 22 (NIV) is supplied by the Greek participle in verse 21. Verse 21, it could be argued, provides the theme for a section which extends to 6:10. The student of the English Bible could very well notice this by observing the repetition of "submit" in verses 21 and 22 but the section heading could cause us to miss the connection — if we are not careful to pay attention to the flow of the text itself.

LOOK FOR "CONNECTING WORDS"

Finally, you should inspect the "boundaries" of the passage being studied for significant *connecting words*. "Connecting words" are words that have special linking or connecting force *between* ideas. They are important because they *create relationships* between ideas. Words such as "but," "for," "since," "when," "after," "so," and "therefore" are important connecting words. They may indicate contrast, motive, evidence, sequence, cause, result, purpose, or some other important relationship. As a result, they are especially important for tracing "flow" between ideas. An oft-repeated proverb of Bible study is to always ask "what the therefore is there for." If you find such words at the boundaries of your passage, try to identify the type of "link" it creates between your passage and the material around it.

EXAMINING REMOTE CONTEXT

Examining remote context is really a job that never ends. If it is true that the eventual context for every verse of the Bible is the rest of the Bible, then anytime we learn something from God's Word we have increased our knowledge of the remote context of any verse. However, placing any particular passage in the remote context of Scripture need not be viewed as such an open-ended task. As much as we may wish to strive for the ideal of a complete mastery of biblical content, it is not quite true that we need to understand *everything* in the Bible before we can understand *anything* in the Bible. It is most important that we avoid the fallacy of the other extreme — assuming that any single verse or passage exhausts what the Bible has to say about a subject. Romans 10:13, for example, contains an important truth about salvation. But, by itself, it does not tell us everything that God asks us to do to be saved. Fortunately, there are strategies and tools which can enable us to locate those other passages in the Bible which have particular relevance for understanding the passage under investigation.

CROSS-REFERENCES AND PARALLEL PASSAGES

An especially valuable resource which many people fail to take advantage of is the **list of cross-references** in their Bible. The "cross-references" are lists of other passages in the Bible which address the same subjects mentioned in the verses under investigation. You might find them listed in the margins of your Bible, in center-columns created for this purpose, or at the bottom of the pages in footnote format. Take the time to locate the cross-references in your Bible. Some Bibles will contain more extensive cross-reference lists than others. The more extensive lists are more likely to help you find relevant passages. At this point remember that, since it is helpful to compare versions as you study, you may want to make sure that you own at least one Bible with an extensive cross-reference list.

To begin your examination of remote context, simply look up as many cross-reference passages as your Bible supplies. As you look up each passage, however, be sure to read *it* in its immediate context! Be sure to read enough preceding and subsequent material to be reasonably confident in your understanding of what has been written. In each case, try to identify any information provided in the cross-reference passage that will help you understand the passage you are studying more closely. The cross-reference may provide additional information that will eliminate some possible interpretations or, in some cases, demand a particular interpretation. The key principle to keep in mind is that since God never contradicts Himself neither will the Bible which He has inspired. At other times, the cross-reference passage may simply restate the same basic idea found in the main passage but it will word the expression in such a way that its meaning may become clearer to you.

Each time a cross-reference passage contributes to your understanding of the passage under examination, make a note of the reference and what it contributes.

A **parallel passage** is a special kind of cross-reference. Some books of the Bible contain accounts of events that are also included elsewhere. For example, many of Jesus' activities and teachings are included in more than one Gospel. In addition to the Gospels in the New Testament, the history books of the Old Testament (1 Samuel–2 Chronicles) often contain parallel passages. Because they present different (not contradictory) accounts of the same events and teachings, parallel passages are often a particularly helpful cross-reference. Comparing the similarities and differences between the accounts provided by different authors can often provide clues as to the purpose or emphasis of each author.

Sometimes the *immediate context itself* will vary — for example, an event recorded in the Gospel of Matthew may be preceded/followed by different material than that preceding/following a record of the same event or teaching in the Gospel of Luke. While our tendency may be to "harmonize" the different accounts, we must remember that each of the writers made strategic decisions about which materials to include and which to omit with the result that the *differences* are actually helpful clues as to the design of the author. For an example, you may want to compare Matthew 6:25-33 and Luke 12:22-31 and the material preceding/following each. Jesus may well have uttered similar teachings on different occasions or Matthew and Luke may each have preserved, in part, a different combination of Jesus' sayings and activities from the same general period of time. Minimally, Luke 12:32-34 would seem to indicate that the teaching recorded by Luke was designed to encourage us to trust God for our own needs and share what we have with the poor.

USING TOPICAL BIBLES AND CHAIN REFERENCE SYSTEMS

In addition to whatever cross-reference passages may be indicated in your Bible, a **Topical Bible** can be helpful for locating other Bible passages relevant to understanding the passage being studied. A "topical" Bible is really an index. Topics (and subtopics) are listed in alphabetical order. Under each topic is printed a list of Bible verses pertaining to that topic. **Nave's Topical Bible** is a helpful and comprehensive tool for such searches. It contains over 20,000 topics and subtopics and over 100,000 references. Hendrickson still publishes the older King James edition. Zondervan publishes a newer edition which is based on the New International Version and which contains new entries reflecting contemporary issues. Ease of use is a real advantage to this tool and it will be especially valuable if your Bible lacks an extensive cross-reference list. However, you will notice that printed verses appear *out of context.* The best way to use this tool, then, is to identify the relevant verses and then look them up in the Bible and read them in the flow of context.

Other study aids are available to assist in this effort. **Thompson's Chain Reference Bible** is available in the King James Version, New American Standard Bible and the New International Version. Its unique chain-reference system can be helpful if you wish to explore beyond the cross-references listed in your other Bible(s). Topics are listed in the margin beside each verse. A "pilot number" is listed to the left of each topic. The reader has two options. She may follow the forward reference printed at the right of the topic. In the following example, we find the topic "Christ Divine" next to Colossians 1:15:

---

g and Prayer

thank God, the
ur Lord Jesus
we pray for you,
have heard of
Christ Jesus and
u have for all the
faith and love
om the hope that
or you in heaven
u be

The Supremacy of Christ

¹⁵He is the image of the invisible God, the firstborn over all creation. ¹⁶For by him all things were created: things in heaven and on earth, visible and invisible, whether thrones or powers or rul...

1314 Forgiveness (1)

4044 Christ, Image of God, Heb 1:3
2490 God Unseen, 1Ti 1:17
702 Christ Divine (2), 2:9 ←
Divine Preeminence of Christ
680 Christ the C...

---

ou, and I fill up in
t is still lacking in
rist's afflictions,
f his body, which
²⁵I have become
y the commission
to present to you
God in its full-
mystery that has
lden for ages and

...to it that no one takes you captive through hollow and deceptive philosophy, which depends on human tradition and the basic principles of this world rather than on Christ.

⁹For in Christ all the fullness of the Deity lives in bodily form, ¹⁰and you have been given fullness in Christ, who is the head over every power

1Jn 1:7
1455 Thankfulness (1), 3:15
Vanity of Philosophy
1797 Warnings (4), 2Pe 3:17
1028 False Doctrine, Heb 13:9
2842 Human Precepts
3652 Tradition, Tit 1:14
3851 Worldly Wisdom

702 Christ Divine (2), 1Ti 3:16 ←
1124 Fullness of Christ†
1123 Spiritual Fullness
716 Preeminence of Christ

The forward reference is to chapter 2:9 in Colossians. Next to Colossians 2:9 we also find the topic "Christ Divine" and the next forward reference is to 1 Timothy 3:16. The reader may follow the forward references in this manner until the chain is exhausted. The advantage to this method is that the reader is able to read each reference in context.

The other option open to the reader is to use the "pilot number." The pilot number next to the topic "Christ Divine" is 702 (note that the pilot number for the topic stays the same — it is 702 for both Colossians 1:15 and 2:9). In the back of the Bible, the reader will find a "Text Cyclopedia" arranged according to pilot number. The reader need only to locate the pilot number to find the complete chain of references assembled in one place, as in the following example:

Possessed before the Foundation of he World.
Jn 17:5 And now, Father, glorify me i your presence with the glory I had ith you before the world began. (Jn 7:24; Heb 3:3)
Ascribed by the Heavenly Host.
Rev 5:12 In a loud voice they sang: Worthy is the Lamb, who was slain, to eceive power and wealth and wisdom nd strength and honor and glory and raise!"
See *King of Kings,* **708;** *Christ Exalted,* 18; *Christ, King,* **3421.**
(H) MISCELLANEOUS TOPICS re- ating to.
684—(1) His Mission, Mt 5:17; 20:28; k 4:43; 12:49; 19:10; Jn 3:17; 9:39; 10:10; 2:47; 18:37; 1Ti 1:15.
See *Divine Messenger,* **694.**
685—(2) His Oneness with the Fa- her, Jn 10:30, 38; 14:10; 17:11, 22.
686—(3) Our Righteousness, Ro 0:4; 1Co 1:30; Php 3:9.
See *Substitution,* **3361;** *Christ* ᵖ
on. 273?

...(1) **A Branch,** Isa 4:2; 11:1; Jer 3:5; 33:15; Zec 3:8; 6:12.
692—(2) A Cornerstone, or Cap- tone, Ps 118:22; Mt 21:42; Ac 4:11; Eph :20; 1Pe 2:6.
See *Spir. Foundation (1),* **3177.**
693—(3) Master, Lk 5:5; 8:24, 45; :33, 49; 17:13.
See *Christ, Lord,* **715.**
694—(4) Messenger, Divine, Mt 1:37; Jn 6:38; 7:29; 8:42; 9:4; 10:36; 17:8, 1.
See *Christ's Mission,* **684.**
695—(5) Messiah, Mt 11:3; 16:16; 6:63; Lk 2:11, 26; 4:41; 24:26; Jn 1:41; :26; 6:14, 69; 7:41; 8:28; 11:27; Ac 9:22; 7:3; 1Jn 5:1.
See *Anointed One,* **677;** *Son of God,* '07.
696—(6) Morning Star (N.M.), Nu 4:17; 2Pe 1:19; Rev 2:28; 22:16.
See *Christ the Light,* **2168.**
697—(7) Prophet, Dt 18:18; Mt 21:11, 6; Mk 6:15; Lk 7:16; 13:33; 24:19; Jn :19; 6:14; 7:40; 9:17; Ac 3:22.
698—(8) Rock of Offense, Isa 8:14; Mt 11:6; 13:57; Mk 6:3; Ro 9:32; 1Co 1:23; 1Pe 2:8.
See *Christ Rejected,* **2965.**

See *Titles of Christ,* **3632.**
CHRIST'S DIVINITY— HUMANITY
(A) SCRIPTURAL TESTIMONY concerning his divinity.
701—(1) His Own Words.
Lk 22:69 But from now on, the Son of Man will be seated at the right hand of the mighty God."
Lk 22:70 They all asked, "Are you then the Son of God?" He replied, "You are right in saying I am."
Jn 10:30 I and the Father are one."
*Jn 10:37 Do not believe me unless I do what my Father does.
Jn 10:38 But if I do it, even though you do not believe me, believe the miracles, that you may know and understand that the Father is in me, and I in the Father."
Jn 12:45 When he looks at me, he sees the one who sent me.
Jn 14:7 If you really know ___ would kno ___ ___ the Spirit ___ rom what is mine and make it known to you.
See *Christ Eternal,* **709.**
702—(2) Testimony of the Apostles.
Mt 16:16 Simon Peter answered, "You are the Christ, the Son of the living God."
Jn 1:1 In the beginning was the Word, and the Word was with God, and the Word was God.
Jn 1:2 He was with God in the begin- ning.
Ro 1:4 and who through the Spirit of holiness was declared with power to be the Son of God by his resurrection from the dead: Jesus Christ our Lord.
Ro 9:5 Theirs are the patriarchs, and from them is traced the human ancestry of Christ, who is God over all, forever praised! Amen. (Col 1:15)
Col 2:9 For in Christ all the fullness of the Deity lives in bodily form,
1Ti 3:16 Beyond all question, the mys- tery of godliness is great: He appeared in a body, was vindicated by the Spirit, was seen by angels, was preached among the nations, was believed on in the world, was taken up in glory. (1Ti 6:15)
Heb 1:3 The Son is the radiance of God's glory and the exact representation of his being, sustaining all things by his powerful word. After he had provided

See *Preeminence of Christ,* **716;** *Christ Worshiped,* **3922.**
703—(3) The Father Bears Witness.
Mt 3:17 And a voice from heaven said, "This is my Son, whom I love; with him I am well pleased."
Mt 17:5 While he was still speaking, a bright cloud enveloped them, and a voice from the cloud said, "This is my Son, whom I love; with him I am well pleased. Listen to him!" (Jn 5:32, 37)
Jn 8:18 I am one who testifies for my- self; my other witness is the Father, who sent me."
1Jn 5:9 We accept man's testimony, but God's testimony is greater because it is the testimony of God, which he has given about his Son.
See *Beloved Son,* **706.**
704—(4) Seven Scriptural Wit- nesses (N.M.)
___ ow who you are—the Holy One of God!"
Mk 3:11 Whenever the evil spirits saw him, they fell down before him and cried out, "You are the Son of God."
Lk 4:41 Moreover, demons came out of many people, shouting, "You are the Son of God!" But he rebuked them and would not allow them to speak, because they knew he was the Christ.
Ac 19:15 One day, the evil spirit an- swered them, "Jesus I know, and I know about Paul, but who are you?"
(B) DIVINE NAMES ascribed to Christ.
706—(1) Beloved Son, Mt 3:17; 12:18; Mk 1:11; Eph 1:6; Col 1:13; Heb 5:5; 2Pe 1:17.
707—(2) Son of God, Mt 2:15; 3:17; 8:29; 14:33; 17:5; Mk 1:1; Lk 1:35; Jn 1:34; 3:18; 9:35; 10:36; 11:27; Ac 9:20; Heb 10:29; 1Jn 4:15.
708—(3) King of Kings.
1Ti 6:15 which God will bring about in his own time—God, the blessed and only Ruler, the King of kings and Lord of lords,
Rev 1:5 and from Jesus Christ, who is the faithful witness, the firstborn from the dead, and the ruler of the kings of the earth. To him who loves us and has freed us from our sins by his blood,
Rev 17:14 They will make war against the Lamb, but the Lamb will overcome

Consulting the "Text Cyclopedia" not only allows the reader to find all of the references printed in one place but permits her to see that the 702 chain is actually part of a larger collection of chains on the broad topic of "Christ's Divinity — Humanity" — (A) Scriptural Testimony, (1) His Own Words (701), (2) Testimony of the Apostles (702), etc. The disadvantage to this method is that the verses are printed apart from their contexts.

The Treasury of Scripture Knowledge, now published by Hendrickson, is yet another alternative. In this work, entries are arranged according to Bible chapter and verse. It includes not only key word cross-references but indicates topical references and parallel passages as well. Nelson has released an updated edition — **The New Treasury of Scripture Knowledge**, edited by Jerome H. Smith. The newer edition contains over 100,000 new references and several corrections.

All in all, these tools may provide an opportunity for investigation which extends far beyond the practical limits of time available for this stage of investigation. In many cases, faithfully exploring an extensive set of cross-references in a good Study Bible will be sufficient. Nevertheless, Topical Bibles and Chain Reference Systems can be helpful devices for opening the whole canon of Scripture to us. In the long run, it will be best to keep your goal in view — understanding the passage which you first set out to study. In the short run, however, there are worse crimes to commit than getting "carried away" when exploring a Bible topic. Few people have been damaged by spending too much time in God's Word.

COMPLETE THE EXERCISE
FOR LESSON FIVE

The exercise to accompany this lesson will continue your investigation of Colossians 1:15-20. **The NIV Study Bible** is a good source for both the cross-references and the outline. You will also need the article on "Colossians" from the **New International Dictionary of the Bible** and **Nave's Topical Bible** to complete the exercise.

LESSON FIVE EXERCISE: EXAMINING THE CONTEXT

Sample Study: Colossians 1:15-20

1. Read the entire letter to the Colossians in one sitting. As you read, list the following:

    a. Any key passages which provide clues to the purpose for writing the letter or the problem Paul was trying to solve:

    b. Any words or subjects that are frequently repeated (include chapter and verse references):

2. Refer back to the article on "Colossians" in the *New International Dictionary of the Bible*. In the final paragraph, you will find a brief outline which divides the letter into four major parts. In which part is your passage found? What might this suggest about Paul's design or purpose for this particular passage?

3. Read the article on "Purpose and Theme" and consult the outline of Colossians in the *NIV Study Bible*. Complete the following:

   a. In your own words, write a theme sentence summarizing the central idea of Colossians:

   b. In your own words, describe the importance of 1:15-20 for Paul's purpose:

4. How does 1:15-20 flow from the preceding paragraph (1:9-14)? How does it prepare for the subsequent paragraph (1:21-23)? Are there any significant "connecting words"?

5. Look up all the cross-references listed in your Bible or in the center-column of the *NIV Study Bible*. List at least three passages that add to your understanding of Colossians 1:15-20:

6. Look up the main topic "Jesus" in *Nave's Topical Bible*. Locate the subtopic, "Deity of." List at least three passages which are not found in the cross-references of your Bible but which add to your understanding of Colossians 1:15-20:

6 ANALYZING THE GRAMMAR

Tools	Skills
English Dictionaries	*Classifying Parts of Speech*
Form-Literal Translations	*Identifying Word Functions*
Various English Versions	*Constructing Flow Charts*

The King James Version of 1 Corinthians 11:23-29 reads as follows:

[23]For I have received of the Lord that which also I delivered unto you, That the Lord Jesus the *same* night in which he was betrayed took bread: [24]And when he had given thanks, he brake *it*, and said, Take, eat: this is my body, which is broken for you: this do in remembrance of me. [25]After the same manner also *he took* the cup, when he had supped, saying, This cup is the new testament in my blood: this do ye, as oft as ye drink it, in remembrance of me. [26]For as often as ye eat this bread, and drink this cup, ye do shew the Lord's death till he come. [27]Wherefore whosoever shall eat this bread, and drink *this* cup of the Lord, unworthily, shall be guilty of the body and blood of the Lord. [28]But let a man examine himself, and so let him eat of *that* bread, and drink of *that* cup. [29]For he that eateth and drinketh unworthily, eateth and drinketh damnation to himself, not discerning the Lord's body.

What does it mean to eat and drink "unworthily"? Since Paul says that the one who does it "eateth and drinketh damnation to himself," we should certainly want to know! Does it describe "whosoever"? Or does it describe the eating and drinking? In other words, is Paul saying that "whoever is unworthy" should not observe the Lord's Supper? Or is he saying that it should not be taken in an unworthy manner?

There are those who suggest that it means the former — that an unworthy person is forbidden to participate in the Lord's Supper. Because they feel unworthy they do not partake. And because they believe that none of us can ever be worthy, they suggest that no one should partake. I distinctly remember, as a young boy, sitting through the meeting of such a group as a goblet of wine and tray of unleavened bread were passed. I watched while each person, in turn, received the goblet and tray and silently passed it on. In the end, not one person had tasted the wine or the bread. We all simply watched it as it passed by!

You may recognize the word "unworthily" as an *adverb*. You might also know that the function of an *adverb* is to describe a verb. It is the function of an *adjective* to describe a noun. "Unworthily," then, does not describe the spiritual condition of the person participating in the Lord's Supper. It is certainly true that none of us are *worthy* of Jesus' sacrifice. This, in fact, is what the Lord's Supper is about — remembering that we are *not* worthy, that we never can be and that this is why Jesus died on the cross! Paul's concern, however, is that we may partake in an unworthy *manner* — as the context of 1 Corinthians 11 suggests, without proper respect for God's gift, without the appropriate concern for other members of Christ's body, and without being preoccupied with physical food. The translators of our more recent versions have sought to make this clear by using the expression, "in an unworthy manner." Regardless, close attention to the **grammar** of the passage could have answered this question for us.

In John 21, we read that after the resurrection Jesus appeared to the disciples by the Sea of Tiberias. In verses 11-15 we read of a miraculous catch of fish and Jesus' question for Peter:

> [11]Simon Peter climbed aboard and dragged the net ashore. It was full of large fish, 153, but even with so many the net was not torn. [12]Jesus said to them, "Come and have breakfast." None of the disciples dared ask him, "Who are you?" They knew it was the Lord. [13]Jesus came, took the bread and gave it to them, and did the same with the fish. [14]This was now the third time Jesus appeared to his disciples after he was raised from the dead.

[15]When they had finished eating, Jesus said to Simon Peter, "Simon son of John, do you truly love me more than these?" (New International Version)

Read verse 15 again closely. The casual reader might simply assume that Jesus was asking Peter whether he loved Jesus more than the other disciples loved Him. And this might well be the case. However, the word "these" is a *demonstrative pronoun*. It is a plural form of "this" which *Webster's New Collegiate Dictionary* defines as "the person, thing, or idea that is present or near in place, time, or thought or that has just been mentioned."[1] Clearly the disciples were near in place and time and had just been mentioned. But are there any other possibilities? What else was near in place and time and had just been mentioned? The fish. 153 of them. This may seem a strange thought at first. But it is possible that Jesus referred to the fish. Especially if Jesus wished to discover whether Peter was willing to continue following Him in spite of the crucifixion and Peter's own denial. After all, Jesus had called Peter to be a fisher of men. But Jesus had found that Peter had returned to fishing for fish. In this particular case, either reading of the text is **grammatically** possible. Sometimes careful Bible study can answer our questions. At other times, it can suggest questions that we've never considered!

Both of these examples suggest that **analyzing grammar** can be an important part of our Bible study. As we seek to further narrow the focus of our study, it is also the next stage of our investigation into the text.

Grammar is the science of classifying the forms of words as well as their functions and relations within sentences. Our analysis of grammar, then, will focus on the structure of the language of the passage. It will seek to identify the form and function of individual words — i.e., does the word "first" function as an adjective or as an adverb? It will also seek to identify the ways that words are combined to form phrases, sentences and even paragraphs so as to form meaning.

ANALYZING GRAMMAR: GENERAL GUIDELINES

Many people are paralyzed with fear over the thought of grammatical analysis. Maybe they still have flashbacks to the days of yore when some grammar teacher with green teeth and forearms like a blacksmith bludgeoned them into unconsciousness with massive sentence diagrams. There is no need here to reopen old wounds nor is an expert command of obscure rhetorical devices with Latin names required. After all, the key is simply *close attention to the details of the text.* Conscientious effort will be more important than precise terminology. The following basic suggestions represent some general guidelines.

BREAK LONGER PASSAGES INTO SMALLER PORTIONS

Rather than attempt to analyze a passage that is several pages long, remember that paragraphs make for excellent units of study. Take advantage of the paragraph divisions of your Bible. If you are gradually studying through a larger portion of text, focus on one paragraph at a time and apply the five stages of investigation at each stage. You can come back to subsequent paragraphs in turn. Since your aim is to go over the exact wording of the passage with a "fine-toothed comb," analyzing grammar can become wearisome labor. This is where you "get some dirt under your fingernails" with the text. Don't set yourself up for frustration by tackling too much at once.

USE A FORM-LITERAL TRANSLATION

Since we are focusing upon the structure of language, this is when a working knowledge of the original languages can be especially valuable. While the authors of our Bible may have been inspired, our translators were not. This does not mean, however, that we do not have dependable translations. Remember that though working with Greek, Hebrew and Aramaic can lend a greater precision to our understanding of the text, we can use our English versions as a basis for close reading with a high degree of confidence. It is only honest, however, to recognize that we are working with translations.

You should keep in mind an observation made in Lesson Three: most of our versions are sufficient for one purpose or another and no single version clearly stands out as the only or best choice for all stages of our investigation. Different versions are useful for different purposes. During this stage of investigation, we should prefer a "form-literal" translation such as the New American Standard Bible, the Revised Standard Version, or even the New International Version. "Paraphrases," such as the Living Bible, or "dynamic translations," such as the Good News Bible, may serve well for other purposes but will not do for this type of close reading. The aim of this stage is to investigate *syntax* — the formal properties of the language employed by the author. Though we may not prefer the form-literal philosophy as a linguistic model for producing an optimum translation, in this case we should prefer a translation that will reflect a sensitivity to the underlying syntax.

COMPARE VERSIONS

From the opening example it is clear how comparing one version (*King James Version*) with another (*New American Standard Bible* or *New International Version*) can help to clarify the function of a word or phrase in a sentence. All versions may be grammatically "correct" but there may be times when one version reads more clearly to us than does another version. Comparing versions can also be a helpful strategy for discovering the kinds of choices made by the translators as they sought to faithfully capture the sense of the original text — and the role that their decisions have played in the structure of the text. In some cases, it might even help you see whether a passage has more than one possible translation! This practice may, in fact, make analysis of grammar more difficult and tentative. Yet if it is true that a passage can be rendered by different structures in our own language, we should want to know that this is the case. Comparing the work of different translators may even help us to discern if a particular version reads more "into" the text than it should.

USE A QUALITY ENGLISH DICTIONARY FOR REFERENCE

People are often surprised to find how much information is contained in a good dictionary entry. Even the person who may not have the slightest memory of the difference between an adjective and an adverb would be surprised to find how easy it can be to tell the difference — and to find out what the difference means. The key is to invest in a quality English dictionary — for example, a **Merriam-Webster's Collegiate Dictionary** or an **American Heritage Dictionary**. For example, next to the word "unworthy" in *Merriam-Webster's Collegiate Dictionary,* we find the abbreviation *"adj,"* which means that this word is an adjective (a table of abbreviations can be found in the front of this dictionary). Near the end of the entry, following the definitions, we find other possible forms of the word. These include "unworthily" which is an *"adv,"* or an adverb. We could also look up the word "adverb" and find that it typically serves "as a modifier of a verb." And we could look up the word "adjective" and find that it typically serves "as a modifier of a noun." A good dictionary can not only help you to identify parts of speech but explain the functions of words as well. No bludgeoning required.

BE SELECTIVE IN YOUR ANALYSIS

If the passage being studied is reasonably brief, one may well have the time to identify the class and function of every individual word in the passage. This would, of course, be ideal. However, if the passage is lengthy enough to discourage such minute examination, some selectivity may be in order. In such cases focus on sentences and phrases which seem unclear to you. It is almost always helpful to "slow down" our reading of long and complex sentences by giving careful attention to each phrase. In addition, you should always examine closely those statements which you know to be the subject of disagreement and for which people offer competing interpretations. Those parts of the passage which receive varied translations should be examined closely as well. The risk in selectivity is that we may not know whether the grammar of a phrase or sentence is significant until we examine it. Nevertheless, some selectivity can help us to invest our time and effort wisely.

KEEP THE BIG PICTURE IN VIEW

Beyond these general guidelines, some specific recommendations about procedure should also prove helpful. Since grammatical analysis emphasizes close attention to details, it may be easy for the reader to lose track of the big picture — "unable to see the forest for the trees" as the overused proverb says. I suggest, then, that you continue to apply a principle that was suggested from the start — gradually narrowing the focus of the investigation. Move from a "bird's eye" view of the passage (i.e., the larger structural "flow" of the text) to a closer examination of the bits and pieces. Beginning with the "bird's eye view" will not only help us to keep the big picture in mind but will also assist us later in the closer examination of bits and pieces.

To bring the big picture into view, it will be helpful to construct a **flow chart** of the passage. While a flow chart is similar to a "sentence diagram" in many ways, it is different in one significant way. Our main concern with the "flow chart" is simply to plot the structure of the text in such a way as to help us visualize its larger patterns. There is no single "correct" way to do this and we should be less concerned about whether our charts are technically correct than we are about our ability to discern the "action" of the text. Any kind of "flow" that will help us see features that were not apparent to us earlier serves the purpose. The chief goal is to help us spot features of the passage that our eyes may not notice at first glance simply because we are not used to reading for them. The flow chart serves to slow down the action of the text and make it easier to spot features which may otherwise escape our notice.

One simple method is to follow the basic "subject-verb-object" sentence pattern. Devote the left-hand side of the page to the subjects, the middle of the page to the main verbs, and the right-hand side of the page to the objects. Any additional nouns, adverbs, and prepositional phrases may be listed in the appropriate "column" directly beneath each main component. Adjectives may appear next to or beneath the nouns they modify — whichever seems most natural to you.

For an example, look up 1 Corinthians 12:4-6 in your Bible. After you have read the passage as it appears in your Bible, examine this flow chart:

```
There        are          different kinds
                              of gifts,
but                        the same Spirit.


There        are          different kinds
                              of service,
but                        the same Lord.


There        are          different kinds
                              of working
but                        the same God
                              who works     all
                                                      of them
                                 in all men.
```

These are rather simple sentences and so some of the key features may be discernible enough in the printed pages of your Bible. Nevertheless, note how much more these features stand out in the flow chart. *Parallelism* and *repetition* make this passage "work." In other words, each of the three sentences employs the exact same structure. Each is a contrast ("but") between what is "different" and what is the "same." Each omits the repetition of the verb in the second clause, bringing the words "different" and "same" closer together, heightening the contrast. The three sentences correspond to the three members of what is often referred to as the "Trinity" — the Father ("God"), the Son ("Lord" is consistently applied to Jesus in the New Testament), and the Holy Spirit ("Spirit"). The "differences" are arranged into three classes — "gifts," "service," and "working." Repetition ("*all* of them in *all* men") brings the passage to its climax. Thus the very structure of the passage — its parallelism and repetition — creates a strong "presence" for similarity in the midst of difference, a similarity rooted in the unity of God's own person and the universality of His work.

This is also a helpful strategy for sorting through the structure of long, complex sentences. In the *New American Standard Bible,* for example, Ephesians 2:14-16 reads as a single sentence:

> For He Himself is our peace, who made both *groups into* one, and broke down the barrier of the dividing wall, by abolishing in His flesh the enmity, *which is* the Law of commandments *contained* in ordinances, that in Himself He might make the two into one new man, *thus* establishing peace, and might reconcile them both in one body to God through the cross, by it having put to death the enmity.

A flow chart might enable you to sort this out:

```
For
He Himself            is              our peace,
    who   made   both groups
                 into one,
    and   broke   the barriers
               of the dividing wall,

          by abolishing
              in His flesh  the enmity
```

```
                              which is the Law
                                of commandments
                                  contained
                                    in ordinances,

             that
                in Himself
             He                     might make        the two
                                      into one new man,
                                    thus  establishing  peace,
             and                    might reconcile    them both
                                      in one body
                                      to God
                                      through the cross,
                                        by it having put
                                          to death  the enmity.
```

The flow chart helps us to see that for all the various coordi-
nate clauses and prepositional phrases which clutter these
verses, there is really only one basic thought: "He is our peace."
The rest of the passage simply explains what this means.

First, we have two further descriptions of the person — He
made two groups one (according to the context, Jews and
Gentiles) and He destroyed the barriers that divided them. Thus
we understand that He is our "peace" in that He makes it possible for people who are different to live in peace with each other.
Next, we have a description of how He makes peace between
these groups — by abolishing in his flesh the enmity between
them. The phrases which follow identify what the enmity is —
the Law (in turn described both as commandments and ordi-
nances). Finally, we find a purpose statement describing what
He intended to accomplish by this act — make the two groups
into one new group living in peace — and how the act led to this
result — it canceled the enmity between each of them and God.
Though the grammar is rather complex, we can slow down the
flow to discern the basic thought of the passage: people can now
live at peace with each other because Jesus' death on the cross
makes it possible for us to live in peace with God.

THE LITTLE WORDS ARE IMPORTANT

Having brought the big picture into view, applying the fine-
toothed comb will still be helpful in most cases. In fact, an

advantage to creating the flow chart first is that it will often make it easier for the reader to pick out significant details. The following list is basic rather than exhaustive but it may keep us from missing important details that we might otherwise overlook.

Knowing the Players

The old adage that "the main thing is to keep the main thing the main thing" can be applied to Bible study. Syntax has a way of placing some people, events or ideas in the foreground and others in the background. Our analysis of grammar should help us to assess the "focus" of the passage and to identify which elements of the text are privileged. To achieve this end we need to keep track of who the "players" are.

The simplest and most common structure for the English sentence is "subject-verb-object." The subject receives the initial and prominent position in the sentence and represents the "doer" of the action or the "possessor" of the object. When forms of the verb "be" are used, the subject is the focus of attention, definition or description. Usually, then, the "doer" is the "main" player.

But this is not always the case. Some sentences use "passive" verbs. Passive verbs use a form of the word "be" along with another verb. The verb most often ends in "ed." "Those who accepted his message were baptized . . ." (Acts 2:38) is an example of a sentence which employs a passive verb ("were baptized"). In sentences with passive verbs, the subject is not the "doer" of the action but the "receiver" or "object" of the action. In such sentences, the "doer" recedes into the background. The focus is upon the one receiving or affected by the action.

In some sentences, it is necessary to identify the "substitutes" in order to identify the players. Pronouns (he, she, it, they, these, etc.) are words that "stand in" for other words — for some person(s) or object(s) named in the nearby context. To be clear about who the players are, we must be as sure as possible about which person(s) or object(s) the pronouns are "standing in" for. As a general rule, that person or object most recently mentioned is the best choice. But at times — as with one of our opening examples — more than one possibility exists. Only the flow of context and clues about gender (masculine, feminine, neuter) and number (singular, plural) can help us make decisions in terms of reasonable probability.

SHIFTING THE TENSES

The players are important, but the verb is where the *action* is. The "tense" of a verb refers to whether it describes a past, present or future action. Often, it is helpful simply to observe the tense of the verb in your sentence in order to identify the time of the action. Sudden *shifts* in the tenses of verbs in successive sentences — or even within the same sentence — are almost always significant. These shifts represent purposeful choices on the part of the writer. Therefore we should carefully ponder what the shift in tenses may suggest about the meaning of the passage. When writing about the superiority of Christ's sacrifice on the cross, the author of Hebrews states that "by one sacrifice he has made perfect forever those who are being made holy" (10:14, NIV). Note the shift from "has made perfect" (past or completed act) to "are being made holy" (present or continued act). Why is it that becoming holy is described as a present, unfinished process if, in fact, our perfection has already been completed? Answering this question is the key to understanding this passage.

Similarly, a key transition in Paul's letter to the Colossians is 3:1 — "Since, then, you have been raised with Christ, set your hearts on things above. . ." (NIV). The connecting word "since" along with a shift from a past tense verb (completed act) to a present tense verb indicates that the accomplished fact of our identification with Christ's resurrection has significance for our continuing way of life. The first event is described as an accomplished fact, the second as an ongoing response. A careful study of context would reveal that this grammatical shift also parallels Paul's shift from teaching to application in the letter.

PENETRATING THE PREPOSITIONS

Prepositions (words like "in," "to," "by," "for," "with," etc.) are perhaps the smallest pieces of our passage. Yet they are often among the most significant pieces since they communicate such important concepts as direction, location, agency, manner, destination, and various other relations. In fact, prepositions are like Volkswagen beetles — extremely compact and often packed to the hilt. Entire volumes have been written to explain the significance of Paul's use of the phrase "*in Christ.*" "Unpacking" prepositions calls for the utmost care. We can easily read more *into* the passage than the author intended to communicate. Nevertheless, with careful attention to context, other parts of the sentence, and the patterns of different authors, it is possible to discern the precise significance of many prepositions.

"Genitive" constructions — *noun "of" noun* phrases — may also require careful consideration. "Of" is a terribly ambiguous word. According to *Webster's New Collegiate Dictionary,* "of" may indicate as many as fourteen alternative relationships. When "action" words are used in genitive constructions, the relationship can be particularly ambiguous. In 2 Corinthians 5:14, Paul writes that "the love of Christ controls us" (NASB). By "the love of Christ," does Paul mean our love for Him or His love for us? Is Christ the "subject" of the act of love (a "subjective genitive") or is Christ the "object" of the act of love (an "objective genitive")? Either case is grammatically possible, although the translators of the NIV ("Christ's love compels us") make an interpretive choice for the reader. As is the case with unpacking prepositions, genitives must be unpacked with caution, paying careful attention to context, other parts of the sentence, and the patterns of different authors.

CATCHING THE CONJUNCTIONS

Like prepositions, conjunctions are little words with big impact. Joining sentences and phrases together, they structure relationships such as cause, result, condition, contrast, and sequence. In fact, conjunctions are crucial in expressing some of the most important doctrines of the Bible. When we examine John 3:16 — "*For* God so loved the world *that* he gave his one and only Son, *that* whoever believes in him shall not perish *but* have eternal life" (NIV) — we see that the conjunctions serve as the primary vehicle of the gospel. What we have here is really a large complex sentence which consists of three shorter "sentences" — "God so loved the world," "he gave his one and only Son," "whoever believes in him shall not perish but have eternal life." The conjunctions join these "kernel sentences" together in such a way as to indicate the relationships between them. God's love was his motive for sending his Son ("For"). Sending his one and only Son was the manner in which this love was expressed ("that" completes the adverb "so"). The result ("that") for those who believe is that they shall not perish "but" (contrast) have eternal life. The motive, manner, result and significance of the gospel are all expressed in the conjunctions of this verse!

ENDNOTES

1. *Webster's New Collegiate Dictionary* (Springfield, MA: Miriam-Webster, 1980) p. 1205.

COMPLETE THE EXERCISE
FOR LESSON SIX

By now, you should be getting fairly well acquainted with Colossians 1:15-20. This familiarity will be helpful and may help you feel less threatened by the challenge of the flow chart. Remember that no one will "check" your homework and, unless you show your charts to someone else or ask someone to inspect them, no one else need see your work. However, you should make the flow chart a priority and use it to complete the remainder of the exercise.

Since reading long sentences and reading with close attention to detail have pretty much become lost arts nowadays, the hands-on work provided for in this exercise will be a crucial experience for you. It may also be especially valuable to consult the exercise notes in Appendix Two in order to see the potential fruits of this type of analysis. It would be best, however, to tackle the passage on your own before you consult the prepared flow chart.

EXERCISE FOR LESSON SIX: ANALYZING THE GRAMMAR

Sample Study: Colossians 1:15-20

1. Using one of the form-literal translations identified in the lesson (KJV, RSV, NASB, NIV), construct a flow chart of the passage in the space below.

2. Examine the main verbs in this passage. What do you notice about them? What might this indicate about the purpose or design of the passage?

3. Circle the following items in your diagram:

   a. All third person singular pronouns ("He," "Him," "His").

   b. Occurrences of words pertaining to completeness ("all," "everything").

4. In a "connect the dot" fashion, draw a line connecting all of the third person singular pronouns. Then draw another line connecting all of the "completeness" words. As you take in the "big picture" all at once, what does the structure of the passage seem to emphasize?

5. Examine the use of prepositions in the passage. Which ones are used? How are they used? How does this contribute to your understanding of the passage?

6. Examine the use of conjunctions in the passage. What purpose do they appear to serve? How does this contribute to your understanding of the passage?

7 DEFINING THE WORDS

Tools	Skills
Concordances	*Identifying Greek/Hebrew Words*
Expository/Theological	*Determining Meaning Ranges*
Dictionaries	*Defining Words in Context*

Someone once said that "words are building blocks of thought."[1] That is, they serve as the most basic unit of human thought, speech and communication. When we choose and arrange our words, we construct the meaning of our message. Since God uses written language (the Bible) to communicate with us, *word meanings* are therefore the "building blocks" of his revelation to us as well.

Now that you have gradually narrowed the focus of your investigation from (1) the sweep of history and culture to (2) the flow of literary context to (3) the structural features of the language of the text, you are ready to consider the significance of the writer's choice of words. You will now want to know, as far as possible, the *precise* meanings of the specific words which appear in the passage. Many people have found that performing "word studies" is an exciting and enjoyable way to enrich their study of the Bible. You might also be surprised to discover the large selection of quality tools available to assist you in your study of word meanings.

Answers to these three questions will help you to define the meaning of a word as accurately and precisely as possible:

- How do words "work"?
- Which words should we study?
- How do we perform the word study?

In the course of responding to these questions, this lesson will also explain how to use several of the aforementioned reference tools.

HOW DO WORDS "WORK"?

This question is so foundational to developing a sound approach to word studies that it must be addressed at the outset. Even before one attempts to define the *goals* of a word study, it is essential to understand how words "carry" meaning.

Semantics is the technical term for the study of meanings. Semantics is a highly specialized field which draws from many different areas of research to explain "how words mean." For the sake of simplicity, however, much of what the beginning student needs to know can be reduced to two basic principles.

FIRST PRINCIPLE:
WORDS HAVE "MEANING RANGES"

Any individual word has the potential to convey any one of several possible meanings. It is a very rare case for a word to have such a restricted range of meaning that it can convey *only* one possible meaning. For an illustration of this principle, simply consult any standard dictionary entry. Only in rare instances is the definition limited to one possible meaning. In almost all entries, several possible definitions are enumerated. For example, consider the many different ways we use a common word like "trunk." When we use this word, do we mean a storage compartment in a car? A piece of luggage? The nose on the face of an elephant? Or the main body of a tree? When we use the word "coat," do we mean a garment that we wear to keep us warm and dry? A layer of paint on a house? The outer shell of a seed? The hair on the body of an animal? In many cases, there may be a shared dimension of meaning at some underlying level — as in the case of the uses of "coat," all of which seem to share a "layer" or "cover" concept. Nevertheless, the *specific* thought conveyed by the word in each *particular* case varies.

Because words have "meaning ranges," we must be careful to avoid what is often called the "single word–single meaning" fallacy. That is, we should take care not to approach word studies in a manner that assumes (1) that a word can *only* convey *one* meaning or (2) that it *always* conveys the *same* meaning each time it is used. Similarly, we must keep in mind that when a word is *translated* into another language, the "receptor" language will not always translate it with the *same* word. This is because it is often necessary to use different words in the receptor language to convey different aspects of the "meaning range" of that word used in the original language.

This all raises another question, however. This question also leads to the second of the two basic principles. If any given word may convey one of several possible meanings, how is it that we understand which part of the meaning range is intended by the speaker or writer?

SECOND PRINCIPLE:
THE MEANING OF A WORD IS DETERMINED BY ITS CONTEXT

The examples above clearly suggest that when we use a word, in any given instance, we do not intend to convey the totality of its meaning range. When we utter the word "trunk," we do not — at the *same* time — refer to a compartment in a car, a piece of luggage, the body of a tree and a part of an elephant's anatomy. With each particular utterance, we intend for our listeners or readers to understand the word as conveying only a part of its meaning range. That is, we mean *either* a piece of luggage *or* a part of an elephant's anatomy. We do not mean *both*.

The clues as to which part of the meaning range is intended are found in the *other* words that surround the word in question — the *context* in which the word is used. Though rare exceptions are possible ("Help!"), we do not use words in isolation. We combine them to form sentences and paragraphs. "Meaning" is constructed in this process of combining. It is only when isolated words are joined with other words that, together, they become intelligible to us as meaning. Words may be the "building blocks" of thought but *meaning* resides in the building created when the blocks are cemented together.

THE TWO GOALS OF A WORD STUDY

A word, then, has the potential to convey a broad range of meanings. Sensitivity to context enables us to understand which part of the meaning range the speaker or writer intends to convey. In keeping with these two principles, it is possible to describe two corresponding goals for investigating word meanings.

First Goal: Determine the word's meaning range. Before we can decide precisely what a word *does* mean when it appears in a verse of Scripture, we must establish what it *can* mean on any given occasion. In other words, we must discover what the *possibilities* are before we can make a decision about which part of the meaning range is most *probably* intended by the writer. To do this, it is important to establish the "boundaries" of the word's meaning range.

Second Goal: Define the word in its context. Once we have established the word's meaning range, we should carefully consider any clues which the context may provide as to the specific meaning intended by the writer. Remember that, ultimately, we wish to define this word as *precisely* as possible — not as *broadly* as possible. Only when we consider how the context of a word *limits* its possibilities for meaning can we avoid another word study fallacy — the "illegitimate totality transfer."[2] It is dangerous to equate the "totality" of a word's meaning range with the meaning intended by the writer in any particular case since (1) this ignores how words convey meaning and (2) we are thus likely to read more *into* a text than the writer intended to convey.

WHICH WORDS SHOULD WE STUDY?

Those who are more idealistic than realistic may wish to study every word in a passage. This would certainly be the most thorough approach and the best way to ensure that we do not miss any possible clue as to the meaning of the text. On the other hand, depending upon the length of the passage, such an approach can become so tedious and protracted that it is no longer the wisest possible use of our time and energy. At the risk of overlooking some potentially significant word, being selective in our word studies may be the more prudent course, especially if we are studying a lengthy passage. To decide which words to study closely, it is best to peruse the passage for words which meet one or more of the following criteria.

REPEATED WORDS

A word that is **repeated** within the passage, the immediate context or with some relative degree of frequency within the work as a whole may be a good object for close study. A quick survey of the passage in the flow of literary context will help you spot such repetition. The initial reading of the entire work in a single sitting should have produced a list of recurring themes or words. Such words tie the passage to its context and to the larger design of the work. Since they were obviously important to the writer, such words should probably receive special attention in your investigation.

OBSCURE WORDS

You may very well find some of words in the text **difficult to understand**. Words that you don't understand don't mean anything at all — *to you*. Whenever you have doubts about the meaning of a word, that word should become a candidate for a word study. If you eventually plan to teach or preach from this passage, remember that if the meaning of a word is obscure *to you*, then chances are it will be obscure *to others* as well. This may provide additional incentive to study such a word closely.

"THEOLOGICAL" WORDS

In one sense, this criteria poses a false distinction — between words which are "theological" and those which are not. Many of the truths of the Bible are conveyed by ordinary words used in ordinary ways, apart from any specialized or "Christianized" definitions. At the same time such words, though used conventionally, can be considered "theological" in a sense because they are the means by which our understanding of God ("theology") is constructed.

In another sense, however, this distinction is appropriate. Sometimes biblical writers *do* invest old words with new meanings. These meanings may not be "new" in the sense that biblical writers detach them from previous convention and usage. But at times the established, conventional meaning of a word can take on a new significance when it is "informed" by a new context. Over time, a word's meaning range can expand, like a tree putting out new branches.[3] The Bible contains many words which have been invested with new significance as a result of being recontextualized within the framework of the Christian faith. The word "faith" itself is probably a good example of such a word. Some of these words even approach the level of technical or specialized theological vocabulary. Words such as "reconciliation," "atonement," "expiation," "justification," "sanctification," "holy," "consecrated," etc., must be studied carefully for their unique significance within God's scheme of redemption.

WORDS WHICH VARY BETWEEN VERSIONS

As you compare different versions of the Bible, you may note a significant variation in the words used to render the meaning of the original text. This is possible because, as we noted earlier, words have "meaning ranges." It is also a sign that there is some difference of opinion — even among translators — as to the best possible choice for expressing the meaning intended by the writer. On one hand, this should challenge you to remain open-minded about what the text might mean. On the other hand, you may also want to study this word more closely so that you can reach an informed conclusion about the most probable reading.

Perusing the passage with these four criteria in mind can help us narrow the focus of our study. As a result we will study those words most likely to yield additional insight into the meaning of the passage. However, once we have narrowed the field of investigation, we need to know what to do with such words.

HOW DO WE PERFORM THE WORD STUDY?

The word study process may be divided into the four stages described below. The amount of time necessary to complete them will depend upon how frequently the word is used in the Bible. As you learn to use the tools described below, you will probably be surprised at what you can discover even without a working knowledge of the original languages.

1. COMPARE DIFFERENT ENGLISH VERSIONS.

You will probably have compared different versions already, but if you did not pay close attention to which specific words receive varied translations you will want to make a list of such words now. It is best to compare as many versions as possible. It is most valuable to consult the "major" translations (New

International, King James, New American Standard, Revised Standard) since they are the most widely read. Consulting a "dynamic equivalency" version such as *The Good News Bible* (Today's English Version) or loose paraphrases such as *The Living Bible* or *The Message* may suggest interesting possibilities as well, but these should be assessed in light of what you discover later in your word study. You should be sure to include the NIV and the KJV in the selection of versions to compare since many Bible reference tools are based upon one or both of these versions.

This first step will achieve two important goals. First, as suggested above, this comparison should help you decide which words in the passage to study more closely. In addition, you should begin to discern the extent of a word's meaning range.

2. IDENTIFY THE GREEK, HEBREW OR ARAMAIC WORD BEING TRANSLATED.

For the vast majority of Bible students, the most limiting factor in their study of the Bible is an inability to examine the text in its original languages. Without a working knowledge of these languages, we are, for the most part, forced to rely upon someone else's translation of the Bible as the textual basis of our study. This is not a critical problem given the number and quality of translations available to us. Remember that the working premise of these studies is that *current English translations, used comparatively, serve as adequate and reliable guides for understanding the Word of God.* A working knowledge of Greek, Hebrew or Aramaic[4] does not provide a magical key which suddenly opens to us the secret mysteries of Babylon.

Nevertheless, the ability to study the original language texts has significant value for adding precision to our understanding of God's Word. Those values need not be discussed here except to note the particular challenge involved in the study of word meanings. Because words have *meaning ranges*, translators will often (1) use the same English word to translate what are different words in the original or (2) use different English words to translate what is the same word in the original.

As an example of the first, consider John 21:15-17 in the NIV:

[15]When they had finished eating, Jesus said to Simon Peter, "Simon son of John, do you truly love me more than these?" "Yes, Lord," he said, "you know that I love you." Jesus said, "Feed my lambs." [16]Again Jesus said, "Simon son of John, do you truly love me?" He answered, "Yes, Lord, you know that I love you." Jesus said, "Take care of my sheep." [17]The third time he said to him, "Simon son of John, do you love me?" Peter was hurt because Jesus asked him the third time, "Do you love me?" He said, "Lord, you know all things; you know that I love you." Jesus said, "Feed my sheep."

Although the word "love" occurs no less than seven times in these verses it does not always translate the same Greek word. In some of these verses it translates a form of the verb *agapao*; in others it translates the verb *phileo*. The same English word is used each time, although it translates, in some cases, a different Greek word.

In other passages, different English words may be used to render the same original word. In Acts 20 (NIV), Paul says in verse 21, "I have declared to both Jews and Greeks that they must turn to God in repentance and have faith in our Lord Jesus." In verse 24 he says, "I consider my life worth nothing to me, if only I may finish the race and complete the task the Lord Jesus has given me — the task of testifying to the gospel of God's grace." The word *declared* (v. 21) and the word *testifying* (v. 24) actually translate forms of the same verb — *diamartyromai*.

As a result, it can be dangerous to assume that, just because you find passages which use the same English word, you have also found passages which use the same Greek, Hebrew or Aramaic word. It is possible, however, to identify the Greek, Hebrew or Aramaic words which appear in your passage and to study their usage — even if you have never studied these languages.

One of the most valuable reference tools for any student of the Bible is a good *concordance*. Basically, a concordance is a word index of the Bible. Using a concordance, it is possible to locate every passage in the Bible where a particular word appears. Concordances exist for each of the major versions listed above (NIV, KJV, RSV, NASB). This study will focus on concordances which (1) are based on the NIV or the KJV and (2) enable us to identify the Greek, Hebrew, or Aramaic words being translated by the English words in each version.

The NIV Exhaustive Concordance, published by Zondervan, is an inexpensive reference tool that any student of the Bible should add to her personal library. **Strong's Exhaustive Concordance**, published by Nelson, provides much the same help for those who prefer to study from the *King James Version*. The methods for using these concordances are basically the same. The instructions below are based upon *The NIV Exhaustive Concordance*.

Using this concordance, it is possible to identify which Greek, Hebrew or Aramaic word is being translated. To do so, simply look up the word which appears in the text of the NIV. The entry for "love" begins as follows:

LOVE (551) [BELOVED, LOVED, LOVELY,
    LOVER, LOVER'S, LOVERS, LOVES,
    LOVING, LOVING-KINDNESS, LOVINGLY]

Ge	20:13	"This is how you can show your **l** to me:	2876
	22: 2	your only son, Isaac, whom *you* **l**,	170
	29:18	Jacob *was* **in l with** Rachel and said,	170
	29:20	a few days to him because of his **l** *for* her	173

The word **LOVE** is the word indexed in the entry. The number in parenthesis is the count of how many times this word occurs in the NIV Bible (it appears 551 times). The words in brackets are related words. Appearances of these words are not included in the list to follow but are listed under the entries for those words. Following the heading is a list of passages in the NIV Bible where the word "love" appears. Each book-chapter-verse reference is followed by a brief portion of the passage. The word indexed is abbreviated by its first letter and is usually in bold type. If the original word is actually translated by more than one English word, the whole phrase which is offered as the translation usually appears in bold type — as in the case of Genesis 29:18. Words that appear in *italics* indicate words which are included to "assist" in the translation but do not appear separately in the original texts. For example, Genesis 29:18 adds the helping word "was." In this case, no such "helping" word is present in the Hebrew text. The Hebrew language is capable of conveying this idea in the form of the verb itself whereas the English language requires the addition of the helping word to express this meaning.

For present purposes, the most important part of the entry is the "number key" in the far right column. These can be used to identify the Greek, Hebrew or Aramaic word being translated. Further down in the entry, one can find the list of references in John 21:

21:15	*do you* **truly l** me more than these?"	*26*
21:15	Lord," he said, "you know that *I* l you."	*5797*
21:16	"Simon son of John, *do you* **truly l** me?"	*26*
21:16	"Yes, Lord, you know that *I* l you."	*5797*
21:17	"Simon son of John, *do you* l me?"	*5797*
21:17	asked him the third time, *"Do you* l me?"	*5797*
21:17	you know all things; you know that *I* l you."	*5797*

You will note that two different number keys appear within these verses. This tells us that although the same English word is used in each case, different Greek words are used. In fact, we can see that in the first two questions Jesus uses one word but Peter responds with another. In the third question, Jesus switches to the word Peter has been using. But what are the different words being used?

The number keys can be used to identify these words as well. Beginning on page 1357, *The NIV Exhaustive Concordance* includes a section titled "Biblical Language Index-Lexicons." The Index for Hebrew and Aramaic words (any Old Testament reference) begins on page 1359. The Index for Greek words (any New Testament reference) begins on page 1572. Using the appropriate index, it is possible to look up the number key to identify the original word being translated. On page 1573 — using the Greek Index because we are studying a New Testament passage — we find number key *26*:

26	ἀγαπάω *agapao* (143)
	love (74)
	loved (40)
	loves (22)
	love (2) + 27
	truly love (2)
	longed for (1)
	loving (1)
	showed love (1)

To the right of the number key appears the word in Greek letters. This is followed by a "transliteration"[5] of that word into English letters. In the parentheses is a count of the number of times this word appears in the Greek New Testament. Below is a breakdown of the different ways this word is translated in the NIV, each followed by a count of how often the Greek word is translated by that English word in the NIV. This word appears 143 times in the Greek New Testament. In the NIV, 74 of these appearances are translated as "love." On page 1803, we find that the number key *5797* refers to the word *phileo* which appears 25 times in the Greek New Testament. The NIV translates it as "love" 13 times, "loves" 6 times, "kiss" 3 times and "loved" 3 times. The number key entries are thus not only able to tell us which Greek, Hebrew or Aramaic words appear in our passage but are suggestive as to the meaning range of these words because they include a survey of the different ways these words are translated and how frequently.

3. SURVEY THE USE OF THIS WORD ELSEWHERE IN THE BIBLE.

At this stage of the investigation, for the sake of accuracy, it is important both to (1) be as thorough as possible and (2) bear in mind the importance of context. That is, you should strive to consult every appearance of the word in the Bible and be sure to look each of these passages up so as to read them in the flow of their own literary contexts (the brief phrase provided by the concordance will be of little assistance here).

Remember that when you are searching for all the appearances of the word, you must focus on the original Greek, Hebrew or Aramaic word. The mere appearance of the same English word is no guarantee that, in each case, it translates the same word in the original language. When consulting the "Biblical Language Index-Lexicons" in the back of the concordance, you should copy (1) the transliteration of the original word, (2) the number key, and (3) the list of different translations. This information will not only help you to locate *all* appearances of this word — it will ensure that you locate *only* the appearances of this word.

The key to this step is to remember that, because the original word will most often be translated by more than one English word, its appearances will be located in several different entries. In the example above, we noted that the word *agapao* appears a total of 143 times in the New Testament. Only 74 of these appearances will be found under the entry for "love," however. To find the other appearances, the entries for the other words on the list must be consulted. By identifying only those references which use the number key *26,* it is possible to locate which verses under each entry translate the word *agapao.*

Keep in mind that the two goals of the word study are to (1) understand the word's meaning range and (2) define the word in its present context. This survey is the key link. The information in the "Biblical Language Index-Lexicons" can be suggestive as to the meaning range of the word. Only by consulting each use in its context, however, can we discern any *relationship* between the various dimensions of its meaning range and the particular context(s) in which each may apply. In other words, simply knowing the various ways in which a word is translated provides neither (1) any *specific* sense of how the word's meaning may vary *from context to context* nor (2) any insight into how the word is used in contexts *most similar* to that of the passage you are presently studying. To understand what a word might mean in the context of the passage you are studying, you must discover — to the best of your ability — both how different contexts affect the sense of the word and which particular sense of the word seems most appropriate for contexts like the one for your passage.

4. CONSULT AN "EXPOSITORY" DICTIONARY.

Even after a close firsthand investigation, it can sometimes be difficult to draw clear conclusions about the precise significance of the word in the passage being studied. In such cases, you should make use of one of the many secondary sources available to assist you. As always and for reasons already mentioned, you should conduct your firsthand investigation before consulting secondary sources. Nevertheless, you should take advantage of the insight offered by those who actually have expertise in the Biblical languages.

An "expository" dictionary is a dictionary of Greek and/or Hebrew/Aramaic words prepared with a view to assessing the significance of their meanings for Biblical interpretation. Many of these have been prepared in such a way that even those who do not know the languages can use them to benefit from the work done by those who do. Because many such tools exist, because their quality varies, and because some tools require more advanced levels of expertise than others, some specific recommendations may be in order.

Because almost all of these tools will employ the *Strong's Numbers* rather than the number keys which appear in *The NIV Exhaustive Concordance*, one simple preliminary step is necessary before proceeding to the expository dictionaries. In the back of *The NIV Exhaustive Concordance* you will find an "Index of Goodrick/ Kohlenberger > Strong Numbers" (beginning on p. 1833). Goodrick and Kohlenberger are the chief editors of *The NIV Exhaustive Concordance* and this index will allow you to translate the "G/K" number into the corresponding "Strong" number. Simply locate your G/K number in the left column and you can find the corresponding Strong's number in the right column.

With the Strong's number in your possession, you are now in a position to access entries in a number of reference tools. Spiros Zodhiates' **The Complete Word Study Dictionary New Testament**,[6] published by AMG Press is an excellent resource regarding New Testament (Greek) words. Entries begin with the Greek word in Greek letters followed by a transliteration into English letters. This really presents no problem for the non-specialist since the entries are ordered by the Strong's numbers. Using the index in the back of *The NIV Exhaustive Concordance*, you will find the G/K number *26* (*agapao*) corresponds to the Strong's number 25. If you look up entry 25 in *The Complete Word Study Dictionary New Testament*, you will find the article for *agapao*. Within the entries, the transliterations are employed which makes them "user friendly" even if you do not know how to read Greek letters. On the whole, the entries in this resource are sufficiently thorough, readable, and reflect a more current understanding of semantics than do some older, more traditional "word study" resources. **The Complete Word Study Dictionary Old Testament** is due in print by the end of 1997.

Presently, the **Theological Wordbook of the Old Testament**, a relatively inexpensive two volume work edited by Harris, Archer and Waltke and published by Moody Press, is a helpful resource for studying Old Testament (Hebrew/ Aramaic) words. Entries are listed alphabetically in the Hebrew language but they can be accessed through a system based on Strong's numbers as well. In the back of volume 2 on p. 1087, you will find an "Index" which lists Strong's numbers and "TWOT" entry numbers. Unfortunately, this creates an extra step for the student of the English Bible. The G/K number must first be translated into its corresponding Strong's number. The Strong's number must then be translated into its corresponding TWOT number. The process is not complicated, however, and it permits the non-specialist to access entries easily enough. As in *The Complete Word Study Dictionary New Testament* described above, entries begin with the Hebrew word in Hebrew letters, followed by a transliteration of the word into English letters. This is followed by a list of "derivatives" (other forms in the same word "family") to which the comments in the entry also apply. The transliterations are employed within the entries.

A less expensive alternative which has been used widely for several generations now has been repackaged by Nelson as **Vine's Complete Expository Dictionary of Old and New Testament Words**. This reference tool actually packages two works into a single volume: *Nelson's Expository Dictionary of The Old Testament* edited by Unger and White and *An Expository Dictionary of New Testament Words* by W. E. Vine. The Old Testament dictionary is included in the front of the book, the New Testament Dictionary in the back. The dictionaries are paginated separately (i.e., Vine's dictionary begins with its own "page 1" rather than continuing consecutive page numbers). Each dictionary is also followed by its own separate index (p. 313 for the Hebrew words in Nelson's, p. 699 for the Greek words in Vine's). The Nelson's index provides page numbers for its own entries (which means that readers can simply look up the English transliteration of the Hebrew to find the page number for that entry in Nelson's) as well as page numbers for entries in the *Hebrew and English Lexicon of the Old Testament* by Brown, Driver, and Briggs (BDB). Using the Vine's index, the reader can look up the English transliteration of the Greek word to find both English key words which can be used to locate the entries in Vine's and page numbers for entries in *A Greek-English Lexicon of the New Testament and Other Early Christian Literature* by Bauer, Arndt, and Gingerich (2nd edition; BAG). I recommend that you avoid the advanced lexicons (BDB and BAG) unless you have some opportunity to study the languages. Otherwise, stick to the Nelson's/Vine's entries.

What many people find useful about this work is that its

main entries are listed under the English words used in the King James Version. Hence, if you work from the KJV (or care to compare it) you can often simply look up the English term used in your passage ("love") and locate the relevant Greek/ Hebrew term (transliterated, followed by Strong's number) within the entry. In the entry for "love," *agapao* happens to be the first entry:

LOVE (Noun and Verb)

A. Verbs.

1. *agapao* (ἀγαπάω, 25) and the corresponding noun *agape* (B, No. 1 below) present "the characteristic word of Christianity, and . . .

If the reader has trouble locating the specific Greek/ Hebrew word within the entry, the index can always be consulted. Of course, be sure to use the appropriate dictionary (Old Testament or New Testament).

Vine's Complete Expository Dictionary of Old and New Testament Words is an attractive reference tool for many because it is inexpensive, it provides data about Old Testament and New Testament words in a single volume, and its entries are relatively easy to locate. As an older tool, however, its contents are somewhat dated, reflecting an older understanding of semantics (how words "mean"). In short, its entries occasionally err in the direction of the "illegitimate totality transfer" and often treat the boundaries of a word's meaning range as rigidly fixed and entirely separate or distinct whereas more recent research has suggested that the meaning ranges of different words often overlap and have a more dynamic relationship to their context. A comparison of the entries in the older work by Vine and the more recent work by Zodhiates for the Greek verbs translated "love" (*agapao, phileo*) illustrate the difference well.

ENDNOTES

1. A. Berkeley Mickelsen, *Interpreting the Bible* (Grand Rapids: Eerdmans, 1963), p. 128.

2. D. A. Carson, *Exegetical Fallacies* (Grand Rapids: Baker, 1984), p. 62.

3. Walter Kaiser, *Toward An Exegetical Theology* (Grand Rapids: Baker, 1981), p. 128.

4. The New Testament is translated from Greek texts and the Old Testament primarily from Hebrew texts, although some portions (Genesis 31:47; Jeremiah 10:11; Ezra 4:8–6:18; Ezra 7:12-26; and Daniel 2:4b–7:28) are in Aramaic, a related Semitic language which employs the same alphabet as Hebrew.

5. "Transliterating" is the process by which Greek and Hebrew words are rewritten using English letters so that those who do not know the Greek and Hebrew alphabets can pronounce the words in terms of their own language. Often, "transliterations" will only provide an approximation of the sounds but this need not hamper one in his study of the text.

6. *The Complete Word Study Dictionary New Testament* is to be distinguished from *The Complete Word Study New Testament* also edited by Zodhiates and also published by AMG Press. Whereas *The Complete Word Study Dictionary New Testament* basically serves as a dictionary or "lexicon" of Greek words which can be accessed using Strong's numbers, *The Complete Word Study New Testament* tends to focus more on the parsing of Greek verbs and grammatical information. A worthwhile tool for these purposes, the latter is, in my opinion, more useful to those who have had some opportunity to study the Greek language. The student of the English Bible who has never studied the Greek language is likely to find much of its commentary somewhat beyond their frame of reference.

COMPLETE THE EXERCISE
FOR LESSON SEVEN

Because this lesson has introduced you to a variety of new tools and several new concepts (some rather abstract), the "hands on" part of this stage of investigation is crucial. The practice and repetition of steps will help to reinforce the most important parts of the discussion.

If you have time, you may want to turn to Colossians 1:15-20 for a brief survey of words before you look at the exercise itself. Applying the four criteria listed above, identify a short list of words that might be good candidates for word studies. Such words might include "image" (how can one be an "image" of something "invisible"?), "before" (in time or privilege?), "supremacy" (a key theme), "fullness" (what would the fullness of God be?), "reconcile" (theologically significant), and "making peace" (theologically significant). The exercise focuses on two words which might be chosen when the criteria are applied: "image" from verse 15 (to clarify an important theological concept — the relationship between the persons of Jesus and God) and "hold together" from v. 17 (since it is translated differently — "consist" — in the KJV). Studying more than one word will require you to repeat the process so as to reinforce your grasp of the procedure.

Developing a systematic, step-by-step approach as outlined above is essential for conducting a complete word study which will yield reliable conclusions. It may be helpful to review the four steps quickly and note that the sequence of questions in the exercise is designed to lead you through the four steps. In each case, you will first be asked to identify the Greek word (1, 6), next to determine its meaning range (2-3, 6), then to survey its use in context (4, 7), and finally to consult secondary sources (5, 8). Questions 4 and 7 will be the most time consuming and challenging. Again, remember that you can check the notes in Appendix Two later. You will need to consult pp. 157, 220, 274, 417, 528-529, 555, 668, 893, 915, 931, 1036, 1089-1090, 1708 and 1794 (not in the order they will be needed in the lesson) from *The NIV Exhaustive Concordance* and pp. 512 and 1344 from *The Complete Word Study Dictionary New Testament*.

EXERCISE FOR LESSON SEVEN: DEFINING THE WORDS

Sample Study: Colossians 1:15-20

1. In 1:15, we read that Christ is the "image" (NIV, KJV) of the invisible God. Using *The NIV Exhaustive Concordance*, identify the Greek word translated "image."

2. According to *The NIV Exhaustive Concordance,* how else is the word translated in the NIV and with what frequencies?

3. List all of the chapter and verse references where this same Greek word is used in the New Testament. Be sure to include every occurrence of the word, regardless of how it is translated (note: you may, for now, omit the occurrence of "it" as *The NIV Exhaustive Concordance* does not distinguish between occurrences of the pronoun by G/K number).

4. Look up each occurrence in its context. Based on this survey, try to describe this word's "meaning range" in your own words.

5. Look up the entry for this word in *The Complete Word Study Dictionary New Testament*. What does Zodhiates suggest about the meaning of this word in the context of Colossians 1? How does this affect your understanding of the passage?

6. In the NIV, 1:17 reads "in him all things hold together." In the KJV, it reads "by him all things consist." Use *The NIV Exhaustive Concordance* to identify the Greek word which is translated differently here. How many times does this word occur in the New Testament and how else it is translated in the NIV?

7. Where else in the New Testament does this word occur (in its various translations)? Describe its meaning range.

8. Read the entry for this word in *The Complete Word Study Dictionary New Testament*. Consider all the evidence you have gathered. In your opinion, which translation seems to best fit the context of Colossians 1:15-20? Why? How does this affect your understanding of the passage?

8 CONSULTING THE COMMENTARIES

Tools	Skills
Critical/Devotional Commentaries	*Reading and Assessing Commentaries Applying Biblical Truths to Contemporary Life*

Now that you have spent several lessons toiling at a close reading of a passage, you are probably anxious to bring some closure to your study. The goal for this final stage of investigation is *synthesis* — integrating the insights and data gleaned from previous stages into a holistic, coherent understanding of the passage and its significance for your life. Such closure may only be provisional. We should always remain open to new possibilities for understanding or applying a passage in light of either new data about the text or our own changing life circumstances. Nevertheless, *some* closure helps us to "package" our understanding of the passage so that it becomes portable and useful for us. Consulting commentaries and moving from exposition to application are ways to create this necessary degree of closure.

CONSULTING THE COMMENTARIES

It will be easier to move from exposition to application if you first bring your understanding of the passage's meaning into sharper focus. You have collected a variety of data about the passage — historical, contextual, grammatical, and semantic. Whereas each successive stage of investigation has gradually narrowed its gaze to more particular aspects of the text, achieving synthesis demands a final "bird's eye view" of the big picture. A primary goal of the commentary study is to help you regain this perspective. This might be illustrated by reviewing the diagram introduced in Lesson Two.

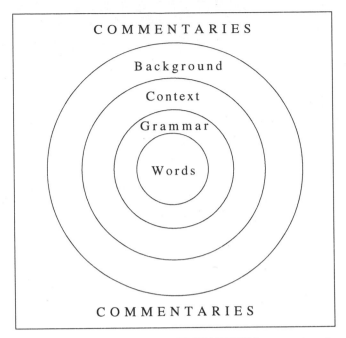

Remember why the "COMMENTARIES" stage is placed out-side of the concentric circles. At this stage, we are trying to "reframe" our understanding by "stepping back" from the details observed through our close reading. We want to integrate those details into a coherent reading of the passage. By "stepping back" and reading the ideas of others, we can gain the necessary perspective to organize those details into a unified understanding. Although consulting a commentary is not a complicated task, you should consider the questions listed below.

WHAT IS A "COMMENTARY"?

A "commentary," as the name suggests, is a book of "comments" on the biblical text. In most commentaries, these comments seek to help us understand the author's intended meaning and, at times, the significance of that meaning for the lives of Christians today. The comments will relate to the same stages of investigation that have been discussed in this book but will often aim at synthesis and, occasionally, application. These comments are the results of the commentator's own study of the text, following many of the same procedures and using many of the same tools to which you have been introduced. Almost all commentators, however, also bring some additional expertise to bear upon their work, enabling them to consult more specialized sources and to conduct further inquiries.

Most commentaries follow a simple format. Usually, a verse or two will be printed (the commentator may reproduce an existing translation or supply his own) with the comments on that verse following. Comments can be looked up by chapter and verse, although most commentaries are more helpful when read from beginning to end, including the introductory chapters.

WHY ARE COMMENTARIES HELPFUL?

Some may wonder why, after conducting a good deal of "firsthand" investigation, they should bother consulting the work of someone else for "secondhand" information. While it is true that commentaries are secondary sources (as are most of the other sources you have learned to use), they reflect many hours spent in the study of a particular book of the Bible — usually far more than most people can afford to invest, either for their personal edification or for preparing to lead others in Bible study. Most commentators are preachers, teachers, professors or writers who have specialized in such study as a part of their vocation. Many are specialists in their field (i.e., languages, history, theology, etc.) and have had the benefit of both advanced preparation and years of experience in working with biblical texts. Hence, the commentary may reflect a wider grasp of the relevant data concerning historical/cultural backgrounds, literary context, grammar of the original languages, etc.

Though commentators vary in the degree of expertise they bring to their task, the old adage "two heads are better than one" almost always describes the benefits of consulting commentaries. It is not uncommon for commentaries to suggest new insights that had not previously occurred to us. Sometimes looking at a passage through someone else's eyes can enable us to see the text from a new or different perspective and to recognize our own biases. Commentaries also look nice on bookshelves and impress people who visit our homes.

IF ALL THIS INFORMATION IS AVAILABLE IN COMMENTARIES, WHY SHOULD I BOTHER TO DO MY OWN WORK?

This question inevitably comes to mind for most students of the Bible. You have learned that Bible study is hard work. Why not simply let the experts and specialists do the work for which they have been prepared and let the rest of us follow their guidance? After all, it's a lot easier to go through the drive-through at the neighborhood fast-food restaurant than it is to cook from scratch — especially when our time is at a premium. Why not settle for McBible study?

Though this shortcut may appear tempting, it is unwise for several reasons. First, commentaries tend to reflect the theological position of the writer. Every person comes to the biblical text with philosophical and theological assumptions and this can affect how he reads individual passages. At times, a commentary may reflect what a writer's theological system tells him the text *must* mean rather than a candid consideration of the relevant data. Second, we must also keep in mind that it is possible for commentators to be wrong. For all of their training and expertise, all commentators are capable of human error. They may neglect an area of study. Their investigation may be incomplete. The diversity of opinions (some contradicting others) is evidence that not everyone who writes a commentary is necessarily correct. We must remember that a statement is not true simply because it appears in print. *Commentaries must be read critically. We cannot evaluate the commentaries we read unless we have first conducted our own investigation. Without prior firsthand study, we are often too easily influenced by the opinions of others.* Anyone who feels presumptuous about questioning the experts should remember that even though the Bereans received Paul's message with great eagerness, they still investigated the Scriptures themselves to see if what he said was true (Acts 17:11).

How Can I Get the Most Out of a Commentary?

Keeping a few "hints" in mind can help you become a "good" commentary reader. First, read several commentaries rather than just one (three to five might be a realistic number). This will protect you from being unduly influenced by any single commentator. It will also allow you to compare and contrast any competing readings that are offered. Of course, the strength of the readings should be tested against the relevant evidence presented for each. Also, remember to reserve your study of the commentaries until you have finished your own investigations. You may find it helpful to consult the introductory sections of the commentaries for background studies but you should refrain from reading the verse-by-verse comments until later. When it becomes necessary to decide between competing readings of a text, your preparation will help you assess the evidence offered. Third, in the course of your study, compile a list of questions which you may later want the commentaries to answer. Your own inquiries may not find answers for all the questions that come to mind and this is one way of allowing your own experience with the text to direct your use of the commentaries. Fourth, remember that the principle of context applies to a proper understanding of commentaries as well as to a proper understanding of Scripture. As you read the comments, read them in order instead of in isolation. Back up and read ahead far enough into the commentary to pick up the "flow" of the commentator's argument. Finally, take notes on important items.

ARE THERE DIFFERENT TYPES OF COMMENTARIES AVAILABLE?

In general, there are three broad types of commentaries. *Critical* or *exegetical* commentaries will focus primarily on a close reading of the details of the biblical text. Most, though not all, will be based on a study of the text in its original language, although the commentary may vary as to how much attention it gives to technical details about that language. Occasionally, a critical commentary may be beyond the grasp of the non-specialist but often this is not the case if the commentary is still intelligible after one "reads around" the Greek or Hebrew.[1] *Homiletical* or *Pedagogical* commentaries are designed to help in the development of sermons or lessons. These may give less attention to the text itself and focus more on suggesting sermon or lesson outlines as well as on the contemporary significance of the text. *Devotional* commentaries are almost always written at a popular level and are easy to read. They will usually focus on application but may offer little in the way of technical data about the text. If you wish to do justice not only to exposition but also to interpretation and application, you may want to consult more than one "type" of commentary. Occasionally, a particularly well written commentary will combine the strengths of more than one of the "types." Any good commentary, however, will always pay adequate attention to the biblical text.

WHICH COMMENTARIES SHOULD I CHOOSE?

Commentaries can be fairly expensive and there are enough of them on the market to consume one's life savings. As a result, you should probably make a common practice of borrowing commentaries and purchasing them only after their worth has been proven. Purchasing a few excellent commentaries that you can depend on for constant use will be far more valuable to you than volumes of second rate commentaries that just look nice sitting on the shelf. Also, follow the same priority in building your personal reference library that you have followed in ordering your investigation of the Bible — purchase the basic reference tools for firsthand investigation before spending a good deal of money on commentaries.

Some commentaries appear as independent works on a specific book (or section of a book) of the Bible. Others appear as a number in a multivolume set of commentaries on the complete Bible (or a complete testament). One or two volume commentaries on the whole Bible are available as well. Remember that the larger commentaries will tend to be more complete and provide more detail, that sets usually include both strong volumes and weak volumes and that a quality one or two volume commentary on the whole Bible might be a good place to begin.

Consult respected leaders within your congregation for advice on purchasing individual commentaries. The list of recommended commentaries provided by Gordon Fee and Douglas Stuart in their book, *How to Read the Bible For All Its Worth* (published by Zondervan), is also worth consulting. **The Zondervan NIV Bible Commentary** is an excellent two-volume commentary which contains the essential contents of **The Expositor's Bible Commentary** (12 vols., also by Zondervan). Another very good one-volume commentary is **The New Bible Commentary: 21st Century Edition** (InterVarsity Press). It is also based on the NIV and supplements *The New Bible Dictionary*. In addition to *The Expositor's Bible Commentary*, **The Tyndale Old Testament Commentary** (InterVarsity) and **The Tyndale New Testament Commentary** (Eerdmans) are very good sets which are available in paperback and relatively inexpensive. Adding these commentaries to your church library would be a practical way for a church to support its members in their quest for biblical understanding.

COMING TO CLOSURE

After gleaning whatever additional insight the commentaries have to offer, you should strive for some provisional closure in your study of the passage. "Closure" means coming to as many firm conclusions as you can about the meaning of the passage and its significance for your life. At the same time remember that you should always remain open to new possibilities for understanding or applying a passage in light of either new data about the text or your own changing life circumstances. Hence it is always necessary to consider your closure "provisional."

A point that was made in the very first lesson of this book deserves to be emphasized again: even though these lessons have focused — for good reasons — on the principles of exposition, Bible study remains relatively fruitless if we ignore the considerations of interpretation and application. In other words, Bible study can — and should — create historical and doctrinal understanding but it will not enable us to please and serve God with our lives until we grasp the contemporary significance and personal life relevance of the text. The field of "hermeneutics"[2] has generated a large amount of helpful literature which explores the philosophical and methodological dimensions of textual "interpretation." In an effort to keep the considerations of this book basic and practical, however, I offer the following three suggestions to assist you in applying the fruits of your study to your life.

First, **paraphrase** the meaning of the text in your own words. This paraphrase should be written on paper so that you have a chance to see it and reflect upon how you have phrased the meaning of the passage as you have come to understand it. You may wish to write your own "Living Bible"-type paraphrase of the entire passage. However, attempting to paraphrase the central thrust of the passage may help you to achieve more focus and clarity in your synthesis. You may want to try to paraphrase the single central idea of the passage in one carefully crafted sentence, using words meaningful to your own experiences.

Next, **describe contemporary life situations** for which the truth may be relevant. Ideas for personal life application may well begin to come to mind at this point, but at this stage you should still be concerned with identifying the broader sets of life circumstances for which the truth of the text may be relevant. Lesson One suggested that there are two primary "means" for identifying present day relevance. Keeping the original historical situation in mind, consider parallel present day situations. Also, attempt to discern timeless truths contained in the passage which are not subject to the contingencies of the situation.

Finally, think of personal life relevance in terms of **beliefs, feelings and actions**. While it is true that any given passage was probably written primarily to instruct us, to motivate us or to persuade us — that is, to address our understanding, our emotions, or our wills — these so-called "faculties" are never so neatly separated either within the purposes of written communication or the human experience. It is therefore legitimate to consider personal life application from all three perspectives. The student of Scripture should always ask these three questions:

- What should I know or believe as a result of what I've studied?
- How should I feel as a result of what I've learned?
- What should I do as a result of what I know and how I feel?

The key to using these questions is to answer them in the first person rather than in the third. While it is relevant, especially for teachers, to be concerned with how God wants to speak to others through this passage, it is all too easy for most of us to apply the passage to someone else without first or ever applying it to ourselves.

ENDNOTES

1.   Gordon Fee and Douglas Stuart, *How To Read the Bible for All Its Worth*, 2nd ed., p. 247.
2.   The more technical term for the art of interpretation is "hermeneutics."

COMPLETE THE EXERCISE
FOR LESSON EIGHT

As you look forward to this last exercise, you deserve to feel good about the diligence you have shown in applying yourself not only to the study of God's Word but to the study of the study of God's Word. To complete this last exercise, you will need to refer to **The Zondervan NIV Bible Commentary** (pp. 819–823). Though you want to devote enough time to the commentary study to do quality research, be sure to reserve sufficient time for prayer, reflection and meditation in order to lay your own mind, heart and life before your heavenly Father.

EXERCISE FOR LESSON EIGHT: CONSULTING THE COMMENTARIES

Sample Study: Colossians 1:15-20

1. Read the comments on Colossians 1:15-20 in *The Zondervan NIV Bible Commentary* (pp. 819–823) and answer the following questions:

   a. How does the commentator describe the problem of heresy in Colosse? How is this similar to/different from your own findings?

b. To which passages outside of Colossians 1:15-20 does
    the commentator appeal in order to clarify the meaning
    of the passage? What do they add to your understand-
    ing?

c. What role does grammar play in the discussion of verse
    16? Does this coincide with your own observations?
    Does this suggest any new ideas?

d. Summarize the commentator's understanding of the following words and compare his suggestions to your own findings:

image —

firstborn —

fullness —

e. Are there any other word definitions which seem important for understanding that were not covered in your own studies? What do they add to your understanding of the passage?

2. As you try to bring your separate observations together into a unified understanding of the passage and to discern the significance of this passage for your life, respond to the following questions:

    a. Write, in one carefully crafted sentence, the main thrust of Colossians 1:15-20. Paraphrase it in words meaningful to you.

    b. Describe at least two contemporary life situations for which this truth may be relevant. Keeping the original historical situation in mind, consider parallel present day situations. Also try to discern any timeless truths not subject to situations.

    c. List at least one of each of the following responses to the passage that should apply to your life specifically:

    A truth or belief —

    An attitude or feeling —

    An action or behavior —

APPENDIX ONE:
BIBLE STUDY SOFTWARE

Those who own a personal computer may be interested in taking advantage of one of the many software packages now available to assist them in their Bible study. Though some packages may impose a few limitations, there are many benefits to computer-assisted investigation.

The limitations pertain to startup cost and tools selection. Though many software packages offer different "levels" or "modules" in which the program may be purchased, the lowest level of entry will almost always represent a small collection of tools. As a result, the startup cost can be higher than when gradually purchasing printed reference tools one at a time. Also, although most of the better packages offer a fairly wide variety of tools, the user is limited to using those tools included with the program (or those which can be added through upgrade modules). If a user wishes to consult a tool that is not packaged with the program, he must either use another/different program which does include that tool or refer to a printed copy.

In almost all cases, however, the benefits of using computer software outweigh the comparatively few limitations. Though the startup cost may be somewhat higher, the financial investment is usually cost effective since purchasing the same selection of tools in print would usually be significantly more expensive. Even though the user may be limited to the selection of tools packaged with the program, the selection will usually bring sufficient benefits from the additional convenience and efficiency in using whichever tools are included. The major advantages are that software permits the student of Scripture to (1) open and consult several tools simultaneously and in quick succession by using either hot-keys or program defined "buttons" and (2) conduct specifically defined searches in a time efficient manner. The processes of conducting concordance searches and consulting cross-reference passages are both made much more simple and convenient.

So many packages are available and so many tools are included that a complete survey of them all would itself generate a major volume. The goal of this brief appendix is to describe a small number of the most popular packages available for the PC operating environment. All of the packages described below are available in versions compatible with Microsoft Windows. None of the packages are particularly difficult to use for those familiar with the Windows operating environment. Tools are used in the same manner as are their print versions, though many of the processes are automated. The manuals included with the programs provide specific instructions for operation.

Logos Bible Software 2.0 is probably the Cadillac of Bible software packages. It is available in four "levels." Each level adds more sophisticated reference tools. Levels three and four primarily benefit those who have the skills to work with texts in the original languages. Level one will be the most useful level to the student of the English Bible. Level one includes the KJV, NIV and ASV texts, *The New Bible Dictionary, The Treasury of Scripture Knowledge, The New Nave's Topical Bible, Torrey's Topical Textbook,* the lexicons and numbers for words used in *Strong's Exhaustive Concordance,* Logos' Bible Maps, a guide to Bible versions and some devotional components (*Pilgrims Progress,* Spurgeon's *Morning and Evening,* and 100 MIDI hymns). This represents a small but good selection of English versions, a good background reference tool, a helpful atlas, the ability to do word searches based upon Strong's numbers, and more help accessing cross-reference passages than you will have time to use. Level two adds the NASB text, *Vine's Expository Dictionary* for more help with word studies, *The Bible Knowledge Commentaries* and *Matthew Henry's Commentary* as commentary resources, Augustine's *Confessions,* and tense-voice-mood codes for verbs. *Vine's* and *Matthew Henry* are both older tools and the tense-voice-mood codes will be most helpful to those who have some working knowledge of the original languages. In addition to the specialized tools for those who can work with the languages, level three adds the RSV text, *Harper's Bible Dictionary,* and *Harper's Bible Commentary* while level four adds the NRSV and NKJV texts and the *Jerome Biblical Commentary.*

A good alternative for the student of the English Bible is the **NIV Complete Bible Library** (otherwise known as **BibleSource**) produced by Zondervan. The most recent version of this package includes the texts of the NIV, NASB and KJV. The selection of tools is based on the NIV text. They include a Bible dictionary for background work (*NIV Compact Dictionary of the Bible*), a topical Bible for cross-reference work (*NIV Nave's Topical Bible*), an excellent concordance (*NIV Exhaustive Concordance*) and expository dictionary (Lawrence Richards' *Expository Dictionary of Bible Words*) for performing word studies, and good commentary material (*Zondervan NIV Bible Commentary* and the footnotes to the *NIV Study Bible*) to consult. Gleason Archer's *Encyclopedia of Bible Difficulties* is also included to provide specialized commentary on difficult passages. All in all, this is a nicely rounded set of reference tools for the student of the English Bible. The complete **Expositor's Bible Commentary** can be added as a module for a very reasonable price. The **NIV Basic Bible Library** is a scaled down and less expensive version of this same package but it does not included many of the most helpful tools. Both packages will work with either Windows 95 or Windows 3.1. The **macBible Library** is a variation of this package for Macintosh systems.

Biblesoft's **PC Study Bible** is another popular package which has recently added some modules to assist those who have original language skills but has retained a selection of tools usable by and beneficial to students of the English Bible. The *Reference Library Plus* includes a small but good selection of English versions — KJV, NKJV, NIV and NASB. The ASV is provided free upon registration. *Nelson's Bible Dictionary* is a solid tool for background research and includes outlines of Bible books. *Unger's Bible Dictionary* is also included and *The International Standard Bible Encyclopedia* provides more detail from an older source. Maps are included as well. *Nave's Topical Bible* and *The Treasury of Scripture Knowledge* help with cross-referencing. *Englishman's* concordances, *Strong's* lexicons, *Vine's* and two advanced lexicons (*Thayer's Greek*

Lexicon and *Brown-Driver-Briggs Hebrew Lexicon*) are available for word studies. An interlinear Bible displays transliterated Greek and Hebrew text with the KJV and *Strong's* numbers. This can cut out a step for the student of the English Bible who desires to quickly identify the word being translated in a passage. The unabridged edition (six volumes) of *Matthew Henry* is included for commentary work.

Bible Companion by White Harvest Software includes a wide variety of tools for student's of the English Bible as well as others that will be more useful to those with original language skills. Fifteen English versions are available (including NIV, NASB, KJV, NKJV, RSV and NRSV). Two Bible dictionaries are included (*Easton's Bible Dictionary, Smith's Bible Dictionary*). Maps are not included although the program does permit DDE access to Parsons' *PC Bible Atlas*. For cross-reference work, *Nave's Topical Bible, Thompson's Chain Topics,* and *The Treasury of Scripture Knowledge* are included. Word searches can be conducted using *Strong's* codes. A.T. Robertson's *Word Pictures in the New Testament, Vine's,* and a selection of Greek lexicons are available to help with New Testament word studies. Commentary resources include *Scofield's Notes, Matthew Henry's Concise Commentary, People's New Testament Commentary, Nave's Commentary, Easton's Commentary,* and *Thompson Topics Commentary.* The precise shape of this package may vary, however, as White Harvest is currently in the process of upgrading their product with a series of three new CDs.

Parsons Technology's **QuickVerse** is a popular package with a low startup cost. The base package includes one Bible translation and *Nave's Topical Bible.* Translations available include the NIV, KJV, NKJV, RSV, NRSV, ASV, NASB, NCV (New Century Version) and The Living Bible. Additional translations can be added later as well as any of the following modules: *Holman Bible Dictionary, PC Bible Atlas, Treasury of Scripture Knowledge, Strong's Exhaustive Concordance* (with Greek and Hebrew dictionaries), *Matthew Henry's Concise Commentary, New Scofield Study Bible, Believer's Study Bible,* and *Expanded Ryrie Study Bible Notes.* Version 4.0 has added a highlighting capability and an edition of *The Rainbow Study Bible.* The cost of modules can quickly add up, however, to a total cost equal to or exceeding other packages.

WORDsearch by NavPress is yet another option, though, like QuickVerse, not as powerful as some of the others. The base package includes one Bible translation and a collection of two hundred maps. Translations include NIV, KJV, NKJV, NASB, NRSV, NAB, The Living Bible, The New Jerusalem Bible and The Message. Additional materials include *The Holman Bible Dictionary, Nave's Topical Bible, Treasury of Scripture Knowledge,* NASB cross-references, *Strong's* codes, *NASB Greek and Hebrew Dictionary, Life Application Notes, Hannah's Bible Outlines,* enhanced *Scofield* outlines, and *Matthew Henry's Concise Commentary.*

There are many other packages available as well and the list continues to grow. Those mentioned above are some of the more popular packages. This brief review may give the reader a representative idea of what is currently on the market, however, and is suggestive as to relevant features to identify when searching for a Bible software package.

You can contact the marketing department of College Press Publishing Co. to find which of their books are available in electronic form at the present time and from which sources.

APPENDIX TWO:
NOTES TO THE EXERCISES

LESSON FOUR EXERCISE:
SURVEYING THE BACKGROUND

Sample Study: Colossians 1:15-20

1. Look up the article on "Colossians" in *The New International Dictionary of the Bible* (p. 227) and find the answers to the following questions.

   a. When did Paul write this letter and what was his situation at the time?

   Paul wrote this letter about the year AD 62. He was a prisoner at the time according to Colossians 4:3, 10, 18. He was probably imprisoned in Rome and had already completed his third missionary journey. This means that Paul wrote this letter late in his life and after several years of missionary service. It was also written about the same time as Ephesians since these letters were carried by the same person (Tychicus).

   b. What was Paul's relationship to the church in Colosse?

   According to Colossians 2:1 it is seems that Paul never preached at Colosse. The church, however, was probably founded by one of his converts during his three year stay in nearby Ephesus.

   c. Who helped to start the church in Colosse and who were some of the other members there when this letter was written?

   Epaphras (Colossians 1:7; 4:12), a native of Colosse, helped establish the congregation. He had just recently come to Paul. Archippus was apparently a leader there at the time of writing (Colossians 4:17). Philemon, to whom another New Testament letter was addressed, was also a member of the church (since Onesimus, his slave, is mentioned in Colossians 4:9; compare Philemon 2).

d. Why did Paul write a letter to this church? Describe the problem there.

Paul wrote this letter because of a report he received from Epaphras. False teachers had infiltrated the church. Their teaching is mainly described in Colossians 2:8, 16-23. It was "Judaistic" (legalism regarding the Jewish law) and possessed a strong "ascetic" (self-denying) element. It could have been a form of "Essenism" or "Gnosticism" but its exact origin is unknown. Paul wrote to refute these errors which apparently had led some to misunderstand the truth about the person and work of Jesus Christ.

2. From the above article, we learned that "Colosse" was the name of the city where the "Colossians" lived. Now use the article on "Colosse" (p. 227) to answer the following questions:

a. How did the city get its name?

The city received its name for a peculiar wool (*colossinus*) produced there. This may have been its chief industry and the reason why it had earlier been a spot on the important trade route from Ephesus.

b. Describe the importance of the city.

Though it was earlier a city of great importance because of its strategic location on the trade route, it later lost its significance when the road system changed. It was soon surpassed in importance by the city of Laodicea.

3. Use the location index in the back of *The NIV Bible Atlas* to find "Colosse" (p. 231). Locate "Colosse" on the map of 1st and 2nd century churches (p. 187).

a. List some of the cities near Colosse.

Laodicea, Apamea, Perga, Eumenia, etc.

    b. Compare the map on p. 186. In what Roman province was Colosse?

        Asia

    c. When was Colosse considered a "significant Christian community"?

        In both the first and second centuries.

4. In *The New International Dictionary of the Bible*, it is suggested that the false teaching at Colosse may have been "incipient Gnosticism" (p. 227). Look up the article on "Gnosticism" (p. 393) and list some of its basic teachings:

- It linked aspects of Christianity with Greek philosophy and Eastern religion.
- Spirit/Matter dualism — God is pure spirit and dwells in the realm of pure light and is totally separate from the dark world which is made of evil matter.
- Therefore God could not have created this world, which is a mistake created by some lesser god.
- Jesus, though he appears to be body and mind, is really true spirit and came to rescue those few people in the world who possess the spark of true spirit by bringing knowledge (*gnosis*) of the spiritual realm of light.
- Salvation is a result of this knowledge which reunites those who have the spark of spirit with the God who is pure spirit.

5. It also indicated that "Colossians" was a letter. Look up the article on "epistle" (p. 319). What does this suggest about the possible purpose of "Colossians"?

As an epistle, it was written as correspondence to deal with a doctrinal or practical situation needing immediate attention. However, the authors realized that, in doing so, what they wrote was authoritative and came from God.

6. Read Colossians 1:15-20. List some of the statements made in the text that may take on new significance in light of the specific historial situation:

- The reference to Christ as the "image" of the "invisible God" (v. 15) seems a direct response to the separation of

God from physical matter (an affirmation of the incarnation vs. its denial). The same could be said of the statement that "God was pleased to have all his fullness dwell in him" (v. 19).

- The statement that "by him all things were created" (v. 16) is a direct refutation of the teaching that God was not directly responsible for creation.

- The fact that God created both "things in heaven and on earth" and "reconciled to himself all things, whether things on earth or things in heaven" also seems directed at the spirit/matter dualism.

- The way of salvation which Paul describes is completely different than the one that was probably being taught in Colosse. Peace with God was made through physical shedding of the blood of Christ on the cross rather than through gnosis.

7. Look up the article on "Firstborn" in *The New International Dictionary of the Bible* (p. 353).

   a. What special privileges did the firstborn son of an Israelite possess? How might these privileges apply to Jesus?

   He succeeded his father as head of the house and received a double portion of the inheritance. Similarly, Christ can be seen as head both of Creation and the Church. "Firstborn" is not a statement of chronology (out of that which was created Christ was the first creation) but of privilege (as Creator, he is "over" — NIV — all creation).

   b. Who is referred to as the firstborn of God in the Old Testament (Psalm 89:27)?

   It is an Old Testament way of referring to the Messiah. In the context of Psalm 89, the stress is again upon His "exalted" status.

8. Look up the article on "Cross" in *The New International Dictionary of the Bible* (p. 241). As you read the description of the act of crucifixion, what stands out to you?

   In relation to what we have already learned, the physical reality of Christ's suffering should seem significant. This was no God who remained isolated from this world in some kind of "pure spirituality" but one who became a flesh and blood human being and suffered a painful death in order to pay the price of our sins in this world. "Peace" with God can come by no other means.

9. Summarize the most important fruits of your survey of the background:

    While in prison, Paul wrote this letter to a church which he had never visited. The significance of the heresies being taught there, however, were clearly considered serious enough to merit his attention. These heresies amounted to a denial of God's involvement with this world — a denial that God created the world, that God became a man in Christ and that the cross was the means of salvation. Instead, it promoted a spirit/matter dualism, the worship of angels, and salvation by an elite form of knowledge (*gnosis*). Upon reflection, the heresies taught there sound surprisingly similar to present day denials of scriptural truth — including claims that Christ was an angel rather than God incarnate (Jehovah's Witnesses) and the various and popular New Age teachings that stress pure spirituality. The truths that Paul affirms here are timely today, then.

    It is also important to understand that the reference to Christ as "firstborn" is a reference not to his status as another created being (as the Jehovah's Witnesses and others teach) but to his privileged, exalted state as head of all creation, the one *through* whom all that was made was made. Central to all that is at stake here is the nature and purpose of Christ's death on the cross, the very way of salvation — the reality of his physical suffering to pay the price of sin and make it possible for us to have peace with God.

LESSON FIVE EXERCISE: EXAMINING THE CONTEXT

Sample Study: Colossians 1:15-20

1. Read the entire letter to the Colossians in one sitting. As you read, list the following:

a. Any key passages which provide clues to the purpose for writing the letter or the problem Paul was trying to solve:

2:1-2 is suggestive regarding Paul's general objective for the area churches (4:16 suggests that the letter was written with the Laodiceans as well as the Colossians in mind) — encouragement, unity, and "the full riches of a complete understanding." 2:4, 8 certainly indicate that Paul was concerned about false teachers in their midst. In particular he seems concerned about the tendencies towards legalism (2:16ff) and the inability of the false teachings to restrain immorality (2:23; 3:5ff). 4:9, 12 also suggest that a secondary purpose was to inform the Colossians of the circumstances of Paul and his fellow workers, particularly their delegate Epaphras (1:7).

b. Any words or subjects that are frequently repeated (include chapter and verse references):

"gospel" (1:5, 23, 23)
"understood, understanding" (1:6, 9; 2:2)
"knowledge" (1:9, 10; 2:3; 3:9)
"wisdom" (1:9, 28; 2:3, 23; 3:16); "philosophy" (2:8)
"mystery" (1:26, 27; 2:2; 4:3)
"redemption" (1:14)
"forgiveness, forgive, forgave" (1:14; 3:13, 13)
"reconcile(d)" (1:19, 22)
"making peace, peace" (1:20; 3:15, 15)
"creation, created, Creator" (1:15, 16, 16; 3:10)
"firstborn" (1:15, 18)
"head" (1:18; 2:10, 19)
"fullness" (1:19, 25; 2:9, 10)
"body, blood" (1:18, 20, 22, 24; 2:5, 9, 19, 23)
"cross" (1:20; 2:14, 15)

The prominence of words such as "mystery," "knowledge," "wisdom," and "understanding" should be regarded as significant in light of what we learned about "Gnosticism" and the Colossian heresy in the previous exercise. Paul's references back to "gospel" and the prominence of words and themes related to salvation, the physical suffering of Christ, the sufficiency ("fullness") of both God's work in Christ and Christ's work in us, and the exalted position of Christ all seem to suggest that Paul saw these heresies as being a threat to the way of salvation according to the gospel which he preached. There is only one way of salvation and it is completely sufficient.

2. Refer back to the article on "Colossians" in *The New International Dictionary of the Bible*. In the final paragraph, you will find a brief outline which divides the letter into four major parts. In which part is your passage found? What might this suggest about Paul's design or purpose for this particular passage?

   You should note that the main body of the letter consists of two sections — a doctrinal section (1:9–2:5) and a practical section (2:6–4:6). In other words, the first half of the letter is designed to teach and explain while the second half is designed to apply and exhort. Our passage is located in the doctrinal section and seems clearly designed to set forth doctrinal instruction.

3. Read the article on "Purpose and Theme" and consult the outline of Colossians in the *NIV Study Bible*. Complete the following:

   a. In your own words, write a theme sentence summarizing the central idea of Colossians:

      Any statement indicating that Jesus' death on the cross was completely sufficient for our salvation would suffice here.

   b. In your own words, describe the importance of 1:15-20 for Paul's purpose:

      It appears to be the most strategic teaching section of the letter. This is Paul's clear affirmative statement about the person and work of Christ that directly counters the "hollow and deceptive philosophy" of the false teachers. Here Paul clearly describes the preeminent position of Christ in both the universe and the church and His work as both Creator and Redeemer. The only sufficient way of salvation is made clear. This passage thus has significance for challenging any teachings in our own day which would devalue the divine nature of

Christ or the importance of His sacrificial death in God's redemptive plan.

4. How does 1:15-20 flow from the preceding paragraph (1:9-14)? How does it prepare for the subsequent paragraph (1:21-23)? Are there any significant "connecting words"?

The preceding paragraph identifies who the "He" of 1:15-20 is — "the Son he loves." It is in this Son that we have "redemption, the forgiveness of sins," a thought which leads Paul to elaborate upon the sufficiency and supremacy of Christ in His role as Creator and Redeemer. It is also worth noting that 1:9-14 ends on a note of praise and thanksgiving — always the appropriate response to a clear understanding of who Jesus is and what Jesus has done for us!

The subsequent paragraph develops the thought of verse 20 in more detail, describing (1) how the death of Christ's physical body makes it possible for those who are aliented from God to be reconciled to Him and (2) the role of faith and firmness in procuring the benefits of Christ's death for our lives.

There are no obvious connecting words at the boundaries of 1:15-20, although the King James Version begins verse 15 with the pronoun "who." This translation is more form-literal but indicates that verse 15 actually continues the same sentence which began in the previous paragraph. Thus the link between thanksgiving, praise and our understanding of the person and work of Christ should be considered quite strong. The "Now" of verse 24 (NIV) probably indicates a shift in thought and the beginning of a new section.

5. Look up all the cross-references listed in your Bible or in the center-column of the *NIV Study Bible*. List at least three passages that add to your understanding of Colossians 1:15-20:

    • John 1:18 (which should be understood in the context of John 1:1-3 is a clear statement of Jesus' divine identity which adds some clarity both to the statements in verse 15 and verse 19).

    • Psalm 89:27 (the title of "firstborn" is used in reference to the coming Messiah).

- Hebrews 1:6 (demonstrates Christ's superiority over angels — he is the object of their worship as opposed to the practice advocated by the false teachers, 2:18).
- Ephesians 2:3 (taken in the context of 2:3-9 — elaborates on the significance of the sufficiency of Christ's sacrifice: salvation cannot be accomplished through our own works but can only be received by trusting in God's grace).

6. Look up the main topic "Jesus" in *Nave's Topical Bible*. Locate the subtopic, "Deity of." List at least three passages which are not found in the cross-references of your Bible but which add to your understanding of Colossians 1:15-20:

- Isaiah 9:6 (predicts that the Messiah will be called both "mighty God" and "Prince of Peace" — the same two themes of Colossians 1:15-20)
- Matthew 1:23 (applies the prophecy of Isaiah 7:14 to Jesus; he was "Immanuel," "God with us")
- John 5:17-23 (the Jews understood Jesus to claim equality with God)
- Philippians 2:6 (clearly states that Jesus was in the form of God and then became a man)

EXERCISE FOR LESSON SIX: ANALYZING THE GRAMMAR

Sample Study: Colossians 1:15-20

1. Using one of the form-literal translations identified in the lesson (KJV, RSV, NASB, NIV), construct a flow chart of the passage in the space below.

The sample chart on the following page is based upon the NIV:

```
He                 is                      the image
                                               of the invisible God,
                                           the firstborn
                                               over all creation.

For
        by him
all things              were created:
things
        in heaven and
        on earth,

        visible and
        invisible,

        whether thrones,
        or powers,
        or rulers,
        or authorities;
all things            were created
                              by him and
                              for him.
He                 is                  before   all things,
and
        in him
all things            hold together.
And
He                 is                   the head
                                            of the body,
                                            the church;
He                 is                   the beginning and
                                        the firstborn
                                            from among the dead,

        so that
            in everything
        He     might have    the supremacy.
For
God                   was pleased
                            to have             all his fullness   dwell
                                                                      in him,
and                              through him
                            to reconcile
                            to himself   all things,
                                            whether things
                                                on earth
                                            or things
                                                in heaven,
                                        by making peace
                                            through his blood,
                                                shed on the cross.
```

2. Examine the main verbs in this passage. What do you notice about them? What might this indicate about the purpose or design of the passage?

    The prominence of the stative verb "is" is noteworthy. It is clear from this that the design of the passage is informative. Earlier stages of investigation suggested that this would be an informative passage which would emphasize the teaching of doctrine rather than action or exhortation. Here we see this reflected in a preference for verbs that serve to identify, describe and define. These are not "action" verbs. Of the other four main verbs, three are past tense and passive. This, too, reflects Paul's focus on the historical reality of Christ's role in creation, Christ's appearance in human history to reveal God to men, and the accomplished fact of reconciliation through the historical events of Christ's death and resurrection.

3. Circle the following items in your diagram:

    a. All third person singular pronouns ("He," "Him," "His").

    b. Occurrences of words pertaining to completeness ("all," "everything").

4. In a "connect the dot" fashion, draw a line connecting all of the third person singular pronouns. Then draw another line connecting all of the "completeness" words. As you take in the "big picture" all at once, what does the structure of the passage seem to emphasize?

    As you "connect the dots," you should begin to discern a type of "mirror" pattern as references to Christ and "all things"/"everything" weave back and forth throughout the passage. It is significant that the passage never allows the relationship between Christ and all things to escape our view. The constant "presence" which this style gives to the completeness of Christ's supremacy reflects the main thrust of Paul's teaching.

5. Examine the use of prepositions in the passage. Which ones are used? How are they used? How does this contribute to your understanding of the passage?

    What is interesting here is the variety of prepositions used and their constant role in introducing the third person singular pronouns. All that happened, both in the acts of creation and redemption, was "by Him," "for Him," "in Him," and "through Him" — the one who is both "over" and "before" all things. The pronouns alone are thus very suggestive as to the completeness of Christ's supremacy.

6. Examine the use of conjunctions in the passage. What purpose do they appear to serve? How does this contribute to your understanding of the passage?

Two items are worth mentioning here. First, the use of "for" to begin verse 16 and verse 19 seems to indicate that Paul is introducing support for the statements which precede these verses. In verse 15, we are told that Christ is "over all creation." How do we know that this is the case? Verse 16 offers supporting proof. Similarly verse 19 offers support for what we read about Christ in verse 18. Thus we see that the passage breaks into two major sections, also marked by the repetition of "firstborn" (v. 15, v. 18). In the first, Christ's relationship to creation is the focus. In the second, Christ's relationship to the church is the focus. In each, a statement of supremacy is advanced followed by support ("For"). Christ's supremacy extends, then, over both realms — over the whole of the redeemed community by virtue of the incarnation, His death and resurrection — and over the whole of the universe by virtue of His role in creation.

Beyond this, it is worth noting the recurrence of the conjunctions "and" and "or." The chart of verse 16 is a good example of how these conjunctions are used to multiply items in lists so as to expand the realm of Christ's supremacy. Thus, the conjunctions create a sense of expansion which gives further presence, in a spatial sense, to the completeness of Christ's supremacy.

EXERCISE FOR LESSON SEVEN: DEFINING THE WORDS

Sample Study: Colossians 1:15-20

1. In 1:15, we read that Christ is the "image" (NIV, KJV) of the invisible God. Using *The NIV Exhaustive Concordance*,

identify the Greek word translated "image."

The word "image" translates G/K number *1635* (p. 555). G/K number *1635* refers to the word *eikon* (p. 1708).

2. According to *The NIV Exhaustive Concordance,* how else is the word translated in the NIV and with what frequencies?

Eikon occurs a total of 23 times in the NT (p. 1708). It is translated "image" 13 times, "likeness" four times, "portrait" three times, "images" once, and "realities" once. Of the three occasions when "portrait" translates *eikon,* two of these translate the word directly and the other actually translates two Greek words — *eikon* used in combination with *echo* (2400). I.e., the single English word represents the presence of two words in the Greek texts. On another occasion, the word "it" actually translates a combination of four Greek *words* — *eikon* and *therion* (2563) used with the article *ho* (3836 twice).

3. List all the chapter and verse references where this same Greek word is used in the New Testament. Be sure to include every occurrence of the word, regardless of how it is translated (note: you may, for now, omit the occurrence of "it" as *The NIV Exhaustive Concordance* does not distinguish between occurrences of the pronoun by G/K number).

image: 1 Cor. 11:7; 2 Cor. 4:4; Col. 1:15; 3:10; Rev. 13:14, 15, 15; 14:9, 11; 15:2; 16:2; 19:20; 20:4.

images: Rom. 1:23.

likeness: Rom. 8:29; 1 Cor. 15:49, 49; 2 Cor. 3:18.

portrait: Matt. 22:20; Mk. 12:16; Luke 20:24 (with *2400* — *echo*).

realities: Heb. 10:1.

4. Look up each occurrence in its context. Based on this survey, try to describe this word's "meaning range" in your own words.

(1) One dimension of the word's meaning range pertains to those "images made to look like mortal man and birds and animals and reptiles" which were the objects of idolatrous worship (Romans 1:23) — these were material copies made to imitate or match the outward physical appearance of the

object represented. All references in Revelation are to the image of the beast which is still an object of idolatrous worship although the power to speak had been breathed into it (13:15). The use of the word in reference to the "portrait" of Caesar upon a coin conveys the same basic idea. (2) Another refers to the nature of man as having been created in the "image" of God (1 Corinthians 11:7, Cp. Genesis 1:27; as in 1 Corinthians 15:49, 2 Corinthians 3:18 and Romans 8:29 of conforming to the likeness of the Son and in Colossians 3:10 of the new self in which that image is renewed) — an idea which similarly carries the concept of likeness but in which the primary concern is probably not material, outward or physical. (3) Yet a third category of use pertains to the relationship between the persons of Christ and God (2 Corinthians 4:4; Colossians 1:15). It is interesting to note that in all three of these dimensions the concept of "glory" (God's glory; man as God's glory; woman as man's glory, etc.) is prominent in the contexts. Perhaps both the second and third categories include the idea of "reality" denoted in Hebrews 10:1 where the word is used in reference to the "realities" of which the law is only a "shadow."

In Colossians 1:15, the outward, material dimension seems appropriate to the context since the word is used as a counterpart to "invisible." Yet it seems that, in contrast to the idolatrous images, an idea beyond that of mere physical resemblance is met as well — after all, God's "fullness" (v. 19) dwells *in* him. Nor does this simply mean that, like other men, He was created *in* the image of God for He is Creator rather than creature. Both dimensions suggest the starkest possible contrast to the false teachers in Colosse who were probably teaching that Jesus was, at best, some flawed imitation or representation of God the Pure Spirit, far removed from that reality in a long chain of angelic mediators. He was the full reality of God present in the finite materiality of human existence — fully God and fully man.

5. Look up the entry for this word in *The Complete Word Study Dictionary New Testament*. What does Zodhiates suggest about the meaning of this word in the context of Colossians 1? How does this affect your understanding of the passage?

He suggests an interesting distinction between *eikon* and its synonym *homoioma*. Whereas both may refer to earthly copies and resemblances of things in the heavens, *eikon* always assumes a prototype, that which it not merely resembles, but from which it is drawn, as in the reflection of the sun on the water or the case of a child who is "possessed of a soul" in the image of his parents. In contrast, *homoioma* involves resemblance or similarity but is not derived from what it resembles, as in the case of two men who resemble each other but are not related. As a result, he suggests that *eikon* indicates the revelatory character of the incarnation.

6. In the NIV, verse 17 reads "in him all things hold together." In the KJV, it reads "by him all things consist." Use *The NIV Exhaustive Concordance* to identify the Greek word which is translated differently here. How many times does this word occur in the New Testament and how else is it translated in the NIV?

   The word translated "hold together" is G/K number *5319* (p. 529). The index identifies the word as *synistemi* (p. 1794). It occurs 17 times altogether. It is most often translated "commend" (6), "commends" (2), or "commended" (1) but otherwise receives a variety of translations including "brings out more clearly" (1), "demonstrates" (1), "formed" (1), "hold together" (1), "prove that" (1), "proved" (1), "short" (1) and "standing with" (1).

7. Where else in the New Testament does this word occur (in its various translations)? Describe its meaning range.

   commend: Rom. 16:1; 2 Cor. 3:1; 4:2; 5:12; 6:4; 10:12.
   commends: 2 Cor. 10:18, 18.
   commended: 2 Cor. 12:11.
   brings out more clearly: Rom. 3:5.
   demonstrates: Rom. 5:8.
   formed: 2 Pet. 3:5.
   hold together: Col. 3:17.
   prove that: Gal. 2:18.
   proved: 2 Cor. 7:11.
   short: 1 Cor. 7:29.
   standing with: Luke 9:32.

This is the same word Paul uses in Romans 16:1 to "recommend" Phoebe as a worthy sister and servant to be received by fellow Christians in Rome. This is exactly how he uses it in the numerous occurrences in 2 Corinthians as he defends his own apostolic "commendation" from God. When, in Romans 3:5, he uses the same word to describe how "our unrighteousness brings out God's righteousness more clearly," he uses the word differently but still with a sense of "public" endorsement similar to that of the epistolary "recommendations." In a similar sense, "God demonstrates his own love for us" by sending Christ to die for us (Romans 5:8) — that is he makes it clear in a public sense for all to see — much as the Corinthians had "proved" themselves innocent and repentant by observable acts of earnestness, indignation, etc. (2 Corinthians 7:11) and just as certain observable acts would "prove" Paul to be a lawbreaker (Galatians 2:18). Paul uses this same word in an almost completely different sense in 1 Corinthians 7:29 — of duration ("The time is short"), although this is quite similar to its one occurrence in Luke which denotes spatial nearness ("stand with"). Otherwise, only Peter uses the word and just on one occasion — when describing the acts of creation ("the earth was formed out of water").

8. Read the entry for this word in *The Complete Word Study Dictionary New Testament*. Consider all the evidence you have gathered. In your opinion, which translation seems to best fit the context of Colossians 1:15-20? Why? How does this affect your understanding of that passage?

   Zodhiates observes that the meaning conveyed by this verb varies according to whether it is used "transitively" (with a direct object) or "intransitively" (without a direct object) and whether it is used of persons or of some other object in a figurative sense. People are introduced, presented, or recommended. Other objects may be shown, made known or proven to someone. Intransitively, the word may mean for a person to stand together with another or, figuratively, to create/bring into existence or to constitute/join together parts together into a whole. In Colossians 3:17, "all things" is the subject of the verb which has no object. Hence it is used "intransitively." The figurative use makes more sense in the context. The creation theme is also strong in the context, although, since Paul has already clearly affirmed Christ's role as creator, it is also plausible that in verse 17 he is describing Christ's role as sustainer — the one by whose sustaining presence the universe continues to exist or "hold together."

EXERCISE FOR LESSON EIGHT: CONSULTING THE COMMENTARIES

Sample Study: Colossians 1:15-20

1. Read the comments on Colossians 1:15-20 in *The Zondervan NIV Bible Commentary* (pp. 819–823) and answer the following questions:

   a. How does the commentator describe the problem of heresy in Colosse? How is this similar to/different from your own findings?

      The commentator notes that "the most dangerous aspect of the Colossian errorists' teaching was its depreciation of the person of Jesus Christ." Specifically, they considered him "only one of many spirit beings who bridged the space between God and humankind" rather than "the triumphant Redeemer to whom all authority in heaven and on earth had been committed" (p. 819). The chart on p. 823 summarizes six aspects of the heresy: (1) Emphasis on worship of angels, called "thrones," "rulers," "powers," and "authorities," (2) Angels are intermediaries between God and human beings, (3) Endorsed submission to the "basic principles of the world," (4) Endorsed circumcision, (5) Endorsed special religious days and legalistic food rules, and (6) Emphasis on a special, secret knowledge. This should basically concur with your previous findings. Note that Paul answers at least three dimensions of this heresy in the passage you have studied (1, 2, 6).

   b. To which passages outside of Colossians 1:15-20 does the commentator appeal in order to clarify the meaning of the passage? What do they add to your understanding?

Most of the cross-reference passages cited in the commentary should be somewhat familiar to you as a result of your previous exploration of remote context and survey of word usages. One explicit aspect of remote context is stressed, however, when the commentator observes about the reference to the reconciliation of "all things" (v. 20) that "one must be careful not to interpret this verse in such a way as to make it contradict the clear teaching of other Scriptures" (p. 821). Construing this verse as teaching a form of "universalism" (the belief that "eventually everything will be brought into a saving relationship with God") is "contrary to those passages that affirm that apart from personal trust in Christ there is no salvation" and to those which speak of the impenitent as going away into "eternal punishment" (Matthew 25:46). The commentator suggests that we understand Colossians 1:20 in a manner similar to the way most people understand Romans 8:19-22 — the main idea being that "all things eventually are to be decisively subdued to God's will and made to serve his purposes" (p. 822).

c. What role does grammar play in the discussion of verse 16? Does this coincide with your own observations? Does this suggest any new ideas?

Your previous study of grammar suggested that the prepositions play a key role in this passage. Your commentator, preferring the rendering of the *Revised Standard Version* over that of the *New International Version*, notes that "three prepositional phrases define the creative activity of Christ": (1) creation was *in* him (he was its "conditioning cause," its "originating center"), (2) creation was *through* him (he was "the mediating Agent through whom it actually came into being") and (3) creation was *for* him (he is "the end for which all things exist").

d. Summarize the commentator's understanding of the following words and compare his suggestions to your own findings:

image —   The commentator does not understand Jesus to be the image of God "in a material or physical sense" or take this as a reference to "Christ's existence in the preincarnate state." The word, he suggests, expresses two ideas: (exact) likeness and manifestation. This is contrasted to "the vague emanations and shadowy abstractions so prominent in the gnostic system" (p. 819).

firstborn —   The commentator notes that this title "may denote either priority in time or supremacy in rank" and suggests that both meanings may be present in the passage. He does note, however, that "the major stress seems to be on the idea of supremacy." He adds that "some see in the word an allusion to the ancient custom whereby the firstborn in a family was accorded rights and privileges . . . He was his father's representative and heir" (pp. 819–820).

fullness —   The commentator suggests that this word seems to have been in current use by the false teachers to refer to the supernatural powers that they believed controlled people's lives. They probably included Christ among a chain of such intermediary supernatural powers through which any communication between God and the world had to pass. Paul, in contrast, suggests that Christ is the one and only Mediator who possesses all divine powers and attributes (p. 821).

e. Are there any other word definitions which seem important for understanding that were not covered in your own word studies? What do they add to your understanding of the passage?

The commentator suggests that Paul's reference to "thrones," "powers," "rulers," and "authorities" (in v. 16) is a possible "allusion to the angelic hierarchy that figured so prominently in the Colossian heresy" although it should not be taken to mean that Paul recognized the existence of that hierarchy of spirits which the false teachers taught. Instead, it should be taken as an affirmation that Christ is the Maker and Lord of whatever supernatural powers there may be.

He observes that the word "dwell," used in reference to the "all fullness" which is in Christ (v. 19), suggests "permanent residence as opposed to temporary sojourn" and that Paul "may be refuting a Colossian notion that the divine fullness had only a transient and incidental association with Christ."

Finally, he notes that the word "reconcile" suggests "removing all enmity between God and the human race effecting in humankind a condition of submission to, and harmony with, God" (p. 821).

2. As you try to bring your separate observations together into a unified understanding of the passage and to discern the significance of this passage for your life, respond to the following questions:

a. Write, in one carefully crafted sentence, the main thrust of Colossians 1:15-20. Paraphrase it in words meaningful to you.

One possibility: Jesus Christ, the eternal God who created and rules the entire universe, died on the cross that I might have peace with God, proving himself worthy of my complete adoration and complete trust for my salvation.

b. Describe at least two contemporary life situations for which this truth may be relevant. Keeping the original historical situation in mind, consider parallel present day situations. Also try to discern any timeless truths not subject to situations.

As mentioned earlier, similar heresies continue to be taught in our own day. Groups such as the Jehovah's Witnesses deny the divinity and lordship of Jesus teaching that Christ is to be identified as a created being, Michael the Archangel, and weakening our trust in Him as the only and all-sufficient Savior. As in Paul's day, we must continue to meet the challenge of false teaching by clearly affirming the truth about the person and work of Jesus.

The identity of Jesus as Lord and Savior and the necessity of completely trusting in Him for our reconciliation to God is a timeless truth that does not change according to time, circumstance or culture. Sometimes our own latent legalism robs us of the joy and peace which God intends to be a part of our saving covenant relationship with Him. We "know" that one can ever be good enough to deserve heaven, that we need a Savior, that we are all saved by grace, and that the cross of Jesus paid the penalty for our sins. Yet often we continue to strive as if there is something that we *can* do and *must* do that will somehow "add" to what Jesus has accomplished at the cross. There is nothing we can add. We can only love and obey in grateful response. This is why the gospel is such good news.

c. List at least one of each of the following responses to the passage that should apply to your life specifically:

A truth or belief —	Jesus is supreme in all ways and His death sufficient for God's saving purpose.
An attitude or feeling —	I am filled with adoration of His person, gratitude for His work, and the joy and peace of the release which His good news brings to me.
An action or behavior —	I will serve Him and obey Him all of my days.

APPENDIX THREE: TEACHER HELPS AND MATERIALS FOR THE SAMPLE STUDY

LESSON ONE: THE "A. I. M." OF BIBLE STUDY

I. "MEANING" AND "SIGNIFICANCE."

II. PRIMARY "A. I. M.":

    A:

    I:

    M:

III. THREE PROGRESSIVE OBJECTIVES:

Objective	Understanding	Benefit	Means

LESSON TWO:
BASIC PRINCIPLES OF EXPOSITION

Five Stages of Investigating a Bible Passage

1.

      A.

      B.

2.

      A.

      B.

3.

      A.

      B.

4.

      A.

      B.

5.

Order of the Investigation

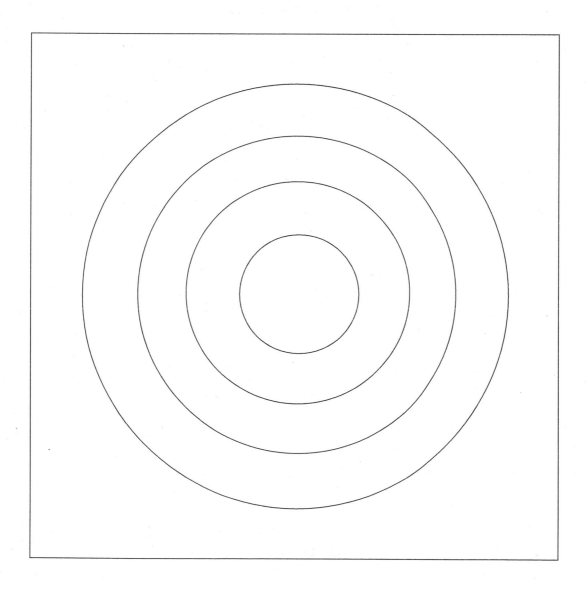

LESSON THREE:
CHOOSING A BIBLE AND A TEXT

Tools	**Skills**
Various Versions of the English Bible	*Selecting a Bible to read*
Parallel Bibles	*Comparing English Versions*
Various Editions of Study Bibles	*Choosing a text to study*

I. Choosing the Version(s).

   A. "Translation" vs. "Paraphrase."

      1. Sources:

      2. Goals:

   B. "Form-Literal" vs. "Dynamic" Translations.

      1. The Form-Literal school of thought holds that to reproduce the _____ *is* to reproduce the _____.

      2. The Dynamic Equivalence school of thought holds that it is often necessary to _____ the form to reproduce the _____ meaning.

      3. The difference between versions is usually one of degree:

Form-Literal   Dynamic

—X———————X———————X———————X—

   C. "Survey of Bible Translations."

   D. Parallel Bibles.

E. Using "Study Bibles."

    1. Benefits:

    2. Risks:

II. Choosing a Passage to Study.

    A.

    B.

    C.

    D.

    E.

    F.

LESSON FOUR:
SURVEYING THE BACKGROUND

Tools	Skills
Bible Dictionaries	*Reconstructing Life Situations*
Bible Encyclopedias	*Determining Occasion and Purpose*
Bible Atlases	*Understanding Specific References*
	to Persons, Places, Objects and Customs

INTRODUCTION

1. Bible study is an _____ experience.
2. Every act of communication originates in a _____ ,
   is addressed to a _____ , and is mediated
   through a _____ .
3. The Bible is an _____ act of communication.

GOALS

1.

2.

3.

I. RECONSTRUCTING THE SPECIFIC HISTORICAL SITUATION.

A.

B.

C.

D.

E.

F.

II. EXPLORING THE LARGER CULTURAL BACKGROUND.

   A.

   B.

   C.

   D.

Tools to Use

   1.

   2.

   3.

For the use of these tools, the teacher may wish to have several copies of the recommended books available for the students' use. Photocopied handouts or overheads may be produced (although care should be taken regarding copyright laws). The pertinent books and pages for this exercise are as follows:

The New International Dictionary of the Bible
       pp. 227, 241, 319, 353, 393

The Zondervan NIV Atlas of the Bible
       p. 231

LESSON FIVE:
EXAMINING THE CONTEXT

Tools	Skills

Outlines of Books of the Bible
A Bible with:
   Cross-Reference System
   Paragraph Divisions
Topical Bibles
	Identifying the Theme and Plan
	   of Book and Passage
	Identifying Connecting Words
	Using Clear Passages to Interpret
	   Unclear Passages

INTRODUCTION

1. Definition of "context":"con" (   ) the "text."

2. Two levels of context:

   a.

   b.

I. Examining the _____ context.

   A. First Step:

      •

      •

   B. Second Step:

   C. Third Step:

   D. Fourth Step:

II. Examining _____ context.

   A. Cross-References.

   B. Parallel Passages.

   C. Topical Bibles.

   D. Chain Reference Systems.

For the use of these tools, the teacher may wish to have several copies of the recommended books available for the students' use. Photocopied handouts or overheads may be produced (although care should be taken regarding copyright laws). The pertinent books and pages for this exercise are as follows:

NIV Study Bible   pp. 1812-1814

NIV Nave's Topical Bible   pp. 521-522

LESSON SIX:
ANALYZING THE GRAMMAR

Tools	Skills
English Dictionaries	*Classifying Parts of Speech*
Form Literal Translations	*Identifying Word Functions*
Various English Versions	*Constructing Flow Charts*

INTRODUCTION

1. "Grammar" is:

2. Grammar analysis focuses on the _____ of the language of the passage.

3. Grammar analysis seeks to identify:

   a.

   b.

I. GENERAL GUIDELINES.

   A.

   B.

   C.

   D.

   E.

II. THE BIG PICTURE (Flow Charts)

1 Corinthians 12:4-6 (NIV)

```
There                    are          different kinds
                                              of gifts,
but                              the same Spirit.


There                    are          different kinds
                                              of service,
but                              the same Lord.


There                    are          different kinds
                                              of working
but                              the same God
                                        who works all
                                              of them
                                              in all men.
```

Ephesians 2:14-16 (NASB)

```
For
He Himself        is              our peace,
    who   made    both groups
                     into one,
    and   broke   the barriers
                     of the dividing wall,


          by abolishing
                  in His flesh    the enmity
                                     which is the Law
                                        of commandments
                                        contained
                                           in ordinances,


      that
              in Himself
          He                      might make    the two
                                    into one new man,
                                      thus   establishing    peace,
      and                         might reconcile  them both
                                    in one body
                                    to God
                                    through the cross,
                                        by it        having put
                                           to death   the enmity.
```

III. THE LITTLE WORDS.

      A.

      B.

      C.

      D.

      E.

LESSON SEVEN:
DEFINING THE WORDS

Tools	Skills
Concordances	*Identifying Greek/Hebrew Words*
Expository/Theological	*Determining Meaning Ranges*
Dictionaries	*Defining Words in Context*

INTRODUCTION

1. Words may be described as the _____
    _____ of thought.

2. When we _____ and _____ our
    words, we construct the _____ of our message.

THREE KEY QUESTIONS.

I. How do words "work"?

    A. _____ is the term which refers to the
    study of "how words mean."

    B. Two Important Principles:

        1. Words have _____ _____.

        2. A word's _____ is determined by its
        _____.

    C. Two Goals of a Word Study:

        1. Determine the word's _____ _____.

        2. Define the word in its _____.

II. Which words should be studied?

    A. _____ words.

    B. _____ words.

    C. _____ words.

    D. Words which _____ between versions.

III. How is a "word study" performed?

1.

2.

- **NIV Exhaustive Concordance**

3.

4.

- **Complete Word Study Dictionary New Testament**
- **Theological Wordbook of the Old Testament**
- **Vine's Complete Expository Dictionary of Old and New Testament Words**

For the use of these tools, the teacher may wish to have several copies of the recommended books available for the students' use. Photocopied handouts or overheads may be produced (although care should be taken regarding copyright laws). The pertinent books and pages for this exercise are as follows:

NIV Exhaustive Concordance

pp. 157, 220, 274, 417, 528-529, 555, 668, 893, 915, 931, 1036, 1089-1090, 1708 and 1794

The Complete Word Study Dictionary New Testament

pp. 512 and 1344

LESSON EIGHT:
CONSULTING THE COMMENTARIES

Tools	Skills
Critical/Devotional Commentaries	*Reading and Assessing Commentaries* *Applying Biblical Truths to Contemporary Life*

INTRODUCTION

1. The goal for this final stage is _____.

2. Ways to create a necessary degree of closure:

   a.

   b.

CONSULTING THE COMMENTARIES

1. What is a "commentary"?

   • A "commentary" is a book of _____ on the _____ _____.

   • Comments can be looked up by _____ and _____.

2. Why are commentaries helpful?

   • additional hours in study
   • specialization
   • new perspectives

3. Why should I do my own work?

   • theological bias
   • human error
   • diversity of opinion
   • need for critical assessment

4. How can I get the most out of a commentary?
   a.

   b.

   c.

   d.

   e.

5.   Different types of commentaries.
   - Critical/Exegetical
   - Homiletical/Pedagogical
   - Devotional

6. Choosing Commentaries.
   - **Zondervan NIV Bible Commentary (2 vols.)**
   - **New Bible Commentary: 21st Century Edition (1 vol.)**
   - **Expositor's Bible Commentary (12 vols.)**
   - **Tyndale Commentaries**

COMING TO CLOSURE

1. _____ the meaning of the text in your own words.

2. Describe _____ _____ _____ for which the truth may be relevant.

3. Think of personal life relevance in terms of _____, _____, and _____ .
   - What should I _____ or _____ as a result of what I've studied?
   - How should I _____ as a result of what I've learned?
   - What should I _____ as a result of what I know and how I feel?

We recommend that the teacher provide copies of *The Zondervan NIV Bible Commentary* for the students' use. Pages 819–823 are applicable to this excercise.

GLOSSARY OF TERMS

commentary A book of "comments" upon the biblical text. Usually a verse or two will be printed with the comments on that verse following. Comments can be looked up by chapter and verse.

concordance A word index of the Bible. A concordance can be used to locate every passage in the Bible where a particular word is used.

cross-reference Another passage in the Bible which addresses the same subject mentioned in the verse under investigation.

dynamic model A theoretical model for translating which assumes that the meaning of the original text is best communicated when it is translated into the natural forms of the "receptor" language, whether this imitates the form of the original language or not. It holds that it is often necessary to change the form in order to reproduce the same meaning in a new and different language. The *Good News Bible (Today's English Version)* is an example of a dynamic translation (it is not a paraphrase).

exegesis The technical term meaning to "draw out" the meaning of a text. Exegetical methods are usually identified with the process of "exposition" whereby we attempt to establish the meaning intended by the author.

expository dictionary

A dictionary of Greek and/or Hebrew/Aramaic words prepared with a view to assessing the significance of their meanings for Biblical interpretation.

form-literal model

A theoretical model for translating which assumes that the meaning of the original text is best communicated when the translation imitates, as closely as possible, the formal or structural features of the original language. It holds that to reproduce form is to reproduce meaning. The *New American Standard Bible* is an example of a form-literal translation.

grammar

The science of classifying the forms of words as well as their functions and relations within sentences. This is similar to what people often mean by the words "style" or "syntax."

hermeneutics

The art of interpretation. The term can be used in either a broad or specific sense. In the broad sense, it is used of "philosophical" hermeneutics to describe how people understand or interpret anything in the world. In a more specific sense, it is used of "literary" hermeneutics to describe how people interpret texts — how they decide what texts mean and discover the significance of that meaning for their lives.

parallel passage

A specific type of cross-reference. A passage which presents a different (not contradictory) account of the same event as the passage under investigation. The Gospels and the history books of the Old Testament contain many parallel passages.

paraphrase   Distinct from a "translation," a paraphrase of the Bible works not from the texts in the original language(s) but from another English version and seeks to render them so as to make them more understandable to the reader. At times, paraphrases seek not simply to "translate" but to "explain" the text. *The Living Bible* is an example of a paraphrase since its primary source was another English version of the Bible — the *American Standard Version* of 1901.

semantics   The study of how words "mean."

syntax   The formal, structural features of a text, i.e., the ways in which words are put together to form phrases, clauses or sentences.

translation   Distinct from a "paraphrase," a translation of the Bible works form the texts in the original language(s) and renders them so as to convey the same meaning in another (receptor) language. The NASB is a translation since, although it sought to preserve "the lasting values of the ASV," its primary textual basis was Kittel's latest edition of *Biblia Hebraica* and the 23rd edition of the Nestle-Aland Greek New Testament.

REFERENCE TOOLS

Barker, Kenneth, ed. *The NIV Study Bible*. 10th Anniversary Edition, revised and expanded. Grand Rapids: Zondervan, 1995, c. 1985.

Barker, Kenneth and John R. Kohlenberger, II, eds. *Zondervan NIV Bible Commentary*. 2 vols. Grand Rapids: Zondervan, 1994.

Bromiley, Geoffrey, ed. *The International Standard Bible Encyclopedia*. Rev. ed. 4 vols. Grand Rapids: Eerdmans, 1979-88.

The Comparative Study Bible. Zondervan, 1984.

Douglas, J. D., ed. *The New Bible Dictionary*. 2nd ed. Downers Grove, IL: InterVarsity Press, 1982.

Douglas, J. D. and Merrill C. Tenney, eds. *The New International Dictionary of the Bible*. Grand Rapids: Zondervan, 1987.

Gaebelein, Frank, ed. *Expositor's Bible Commentary*. 12 vols. Grand Rapids: Zondervan, 1979-90.

Harris, R. Laird, Gleason L. Archer and Bruce K. Waltke. *Theological Wordbook of the Old Testament*. 2 vols. Chicago: Moody Press, 1980.

Kohlenberger, John R. II and Edward Goodrick, eds. *The NIV Exhaustive Concordance*. Grand Rapids: Zondervan, 1990.

The Layman's Parallel Bible. Zondervan, 1981.

Mish, Frederick C., ed. *Merriam-Webster's Collegiate Dictionary*. 10th ed. Springfield, MA: Merriam-Webster, 1993.

Morris, Leon, ed. *The Tyndale New Testament Commentaries*. Grand Rapids: Eerdmans, 1975ff.

Morris, William, ed. *American Heritage Dictionary of the English Language*. College Edition. Boston: Houghton-Mifflin, 1986.

Nave, Orville J. *Nave's Topical Bible*. Rev. by Edward Viening. Grand Rapids: Zondervan, c. 1969.

Newfeldt, ed. *Webster's New World Dictionary: 4th College Edition*. New York: Macmillan, 1997

Paterson, John H., Donald J. Wiseman and John J. Bimson, eds. *The New Bible Atlas*. Downers Grove, IL: InterVarsity Press, 1994.

Rasmussen, Carl. *Zondervan NIV Atlas of the Bible*. Grand Rapids: Zondervan, 1989.

Smith, Jerome, ed. *The New Treasury of Scripture Knowledge*. Nashville: Nelson, 1992.

Strong, James. *Strong's Exhaustive Concordance*. Grand Rapids: Baker, 1989.

Tenney, Merrill C., ed. *The Zondervan Pictorial Bible Encyclopedia*. 5 vols. Grand Rapids: Zondervan, 1980.

Thompson, F. G. *Thompson's Chain Reference Bible*. B. B. Kirkbride Bible Co., c. 1989 (KJV), c. 1990 (NIV), c. 1993 (NASB).

Wenham, G. J., J. A. Motyer, D. A. Carson and R. T. France, eds. *New Bible Commentary: 21st Century Edition*. Downers Grove, IL: InterVarsity Press, 1994.

Wiseman, Donald J., ed. The *Tyndale Old Testament Commentaries*. Downers Grove, IL: InterVarsity Press, 1981.

Vine, W. E., Merrill F. Unger, and William White, Jr. *Vine's Complete Expository Dictionary of Old and New Testament Words*. Nashville: Nelson, 1985.

Zodhiates, Spiros. *The Complete Word Study Dictionary New Testament*. Chattanooga, TN: AMG Press, 1992.